MW00982111

DANCING WITH FATE

Tom and Bette spurn Rommel and the Blitz

Ken Swan

◆ FriesenPress

Suite 300 - 990 Fort St
Victoria, BC, Canada, V8V 3K2
www.friesenpress.com

Copyright © 2015 by Ken Swan
First Edition — 2015

All rights reserved.

No part of this publication may be reproduced in any form, or by
any means, electronic or mechanical, including photocopying,
recording, or any information browsing, storage, or retrieval
system, without permission in writing from FriesenPress.

ISBN
978-1-4602-7172-8 (Hardcover)
978-1-4602-7173-5 (Paperback)
978-1-4602-7174-2 (eBook)

1. Biography & Autobiography, Military

Distributed to the trade by The Ingram Book Company

TABLE OF CONTENTS

ACKNOWLEDGMENTS

I owe a special debt of gratitude to two people who helped me write this book. The first is Sylvia Taylor, Wordsmith and an author, who lives here in White Rock. She made me work efficiently and helped guide me through the minefields of writing my first book.

I also have to thank Tom Grant who is an author and producer of magnificent photographic books. Tom lives nearby in Vancouver. I had a shoebox filled with old photographs, some of which were cracked, dog-eared and almost worthless. Tom not only rescued the pictures, he also contributed some great ideas to include in the book.

DEDICATION

This book is dedicated to my sister, Mary Hughes. She had written a book about her religious beliefs and one day started to "nag" at me to get started on my book. Mary had looked after Aunty Bette in her home and then the care-centre for the last three or four years of Bette's life. During those years Mary would ask Bette for information, usually at my request. I would ask for say, "the name of the church". Or "what car did she own", and so on.

Mary was the perfect detective and fed me with information I was missing. She told Bette I was writing this book and she liked that idea. She found photos that are included in this book, so readers can get to see who the characters are.

I sent my manuscript to Mary in January 2015; she loved it. Sadly Mary died on March 5th 2015 so never got to see, hold and read the actual book.

Thanks, Mary, your nagging and your info-gathering efforts made the book easier to write.

AUTHOR'S NOTES

I spent most of my early years with my mother, being carried from one air raid bomb shelter to another, during World War II. The "Blitz" was the word given to the German bombing campaign against London and surrounding areas. The first bomb was dropped well before my birth, ironically on August 24 1940; I was born on August 24 1941. The bombing had eased off a little by the end of May 1941, but never really stopped throughout the war. We lived, mostly, in a small brick semi-detached house in Stoke-Gifford, a neighbourhood, outside Bristol, England with occasional nightly visits to safer places. At least the assumption was that those other places were safer.

My father, Charles Swan, born in London in 1911. He was the oldest of five children; Elizabeth (Bette) was his sister. He was in the Royal Marine Commandos after spending his earlier years working for the Bristol Airplane Company. He was involved in hand to hand combat in World War II, and helped annoy the Germans by sabotaging railways and ammunition dumps. He helped free prisoners who were being guarded at camps, waiting to transfer to a permanent POW camp. That's all I knew and I had to drag that out of my Uncle George. My father never talked about the war so I cannot write of him.

Uncle Tom, on the other hand, relished my curiosity and told me first-hand what you are about to read. He wrote some of his observations on lined pads, in a scrawl of penciled upper case print with pages of two or three line sentences for each episode.

My mother, Mary Agnes Dowdall, was born in Dublin, Ireland, in 1910, She emigrated to England with her parents in 1916. After school she became a nurse in Manchester around 1935. Four-foot-ten with sparkling blue eyes and a gleeful sense of humour. She met my father while he was guarding a hole in which an undetonated British bomb from a failed practice run resided. She was coming home after a midnight shift, in 1938. She tried to step over the rope that had a big sign stating "Do not cross." She persuaded my father to let her through as it would be a very long detour for her to walk around. "Well," he said, "it's all okay if I hold the rope." An executive decision that paid off.

We came out of the war unscathed but with an imprint on me. I am left with a deep understanding of what ordinary people had to endure when faced with adversity. The Germans paid scant attention to an upstart named Hitler. They got what they didn't want. A lesson for us all today.

Humour was a trait of the average Brit, used to diffuse the pain and never ending nuisance, sadness and horror of the nightly bombing and the loss of loved ones. My mother said, "I am sure Hitler has my diary. No matter where we move to seek safety, he bombs us that night." I of course do not remember specifics but in one week we moved from Bristol to Plymouth, just up the South Coast, we were bombed. Then to my Aunt Tessa's home in Glamorgan, Wales for just one night; we were bombed. Then on to London to stay at Aunt Bette's flat and each night we were bombed. Many nights our bedroom was a platform in an Underground Railway Station, when we were living closer to London. All that experience, at such a young age led me to many war-time skills; I could distinguish the difference between enemy or friendly planes by their engine sound. However it was a skill the war department never called on me to use.

You will see what Bette had to endure and how Tom spent his war years. Then how the two met again after the war. This may be just another war story for some, and it is. But for me it is also an opportunity to thank Tom for his efforts. He contributed very little, he told me, but the combined efforts of all those others who also say they too did very little, were the reason the allies' efforts helped beat what the axis put together to try and rule us. Tom just did his part. He was not a hero but in total his story is noteworthy. Every soldier had stories, but Tom sure had more than a few, and beyond 'normal'. Good for you Tom, and Bette, and all you others who formed what were called 'the allies', Thank you. And for all you readers, enjoy the book.

I have thought about writing this book for decades and now seems just the right time to get it finished before I too disappear and who would know about all these exploits. I tried many sources and methods of research but few ever responded. Watch those sources come out of the woodwork now! It's a good thing I wrote down notes? With both Bette and Tom gone, the notes are all I have along with some press clippings and Tom's army pay book. The dialogues in this book are based on Tom's memory and mine and Bette's. Who knows what was actually said when two people were alone together? I believe they are pretty damn close to what really was said and done.

A number of locations and dates, along with a few names, have been changed so as to help the storyline and make it move along a little smoother. Actual military units, especially the axis in North Africa, are too complicated to use. Their absence does not hinder the stories. Family names are accurate. The changes take away nothing from the facts. Any reader who believes they were the character described here-in please enjoy the story's and tell all your friends. Nobody else wrote about your imagination before you think I did.

This story is based on true facts. Some of the battle descriptions are a composite of real battles. Many of the characters named are composites of people who really existed. Dialogue was based on a composite of Tom's recollection, but created to help establish the storyline.

I was asked to explain military time, or the 24 hour clock time, by a number of readers of my first manuscripts. It is essentially used by the military and, as much of this book is about war and so on, then it is an important inclusion. It is easier and quicker to understand once one understands it. A day has 24 hours. 12 o'clock noon is 12 hours after midnight so it is 1200. Midnight is 2400. One minute after midnight is 0001. Use normal hours up to noon, then just add on the time to 12 after noon. So 3:00 p.m. is 3 hours past noon so 1200 + 3 is 1500. 8:00 p.m. is 1200 + 8 hours later which is? Yes! 2000 hours. Once you get the hang of it, it's easy.

Ken Swan
–White Rock, British Columbia, Canada. June, 2015

1

A REALLY BAD DAY

Elizabeth Swan married Jack Simmons on 10 December, 1941. The wartime wedding ceremony had just ended less than ten minutes before in St. Marks, Kennington, in a lower middle class area of London, England, just off Camberwell Road. This was the East End of London, where, seemingly, the Germans preferred to drop their bombs every night. The pilots found the area easily, aimed for the docks and any near misses hit Clapham and surrounds. Finding one's way around wartime London and finding buildings not only standing, but parts of them still functioning, was quite a feat. Somehow Bette managed to arrange the wedding and the buildings were spared, at least until Bette had done with them. When Bette wanted something done she did it herself and always got it done, and done correctly. Bette was aged twenty-eight and nearly 5 foot 8". She was strong boned and willed and weighed about 140 pounds. Jack was a

Royal Navy sailor, aged twenty-nine, a little taller than Bette and lanky. He had no special rank, like thousands of other sailors, he was simply working to get rid of Adolf Hitler.

Bette was born near The Swan Pub in Stockwell, London, England, and worked at a cleaning establishment, near Marble Arch, as a bookkeeper. Jack had been given a weekend pass to get married, which meant the couple had about thirty six hours for a honeymoon, which they had planned to enjoy in the Belgrave hotel opposite the Brown Derby on Elias Lane. They planned a quick walk over the road to quaff down some refreshing drinks. The Belgrave was a bit posh but as Bette said, "Marriage is only once in a lifetime".

Twenty-one friends, including Bette's mother and two younger sisters, Edie and Lily, both of whom were bridesmaids, attended. (Bette's father, my Grandfather, a Southern Railways steam engine driver, had died about eight years prior from pneumonia and sadly, could not give away his daughter). George, Bette's younger brother and his wife, Pat, were there. And so was her best friend Kitty Gale.

Bette wore a beautiful white wedding gown, as did her two bridesmaids. Jack wore his dress Navy uniform. The ladies all had very fashionable hairstyles with wavy curls over their heads to reach up to their small stylish forties look hats. Of course, frocks were just below the knee and most women had on boleros or suits. Nylon stockings were scarce but which could be afforded on the black market by not eating meat for two weeks. Of course the seams were precisely down the back of the leg and they wore the latest high heeled shoes. Some men in attendance had three piece suits of heavy serge, white shirts with studded removable collars, rigid with starch and with shoes gleaming with Nugget polish. Any polish not on their shoes could likely be found on an old piece of newspaper back home still on the kitchen table or spotted all over the lino on the kitchen floor. All the other men were in some military uniform.

While all this was happening I was four months old and getting excited because it was my feeding time back in Bristol.

The small crowd was about to cross the road to go to the Brown Derby for a celebratory drink when a military dispatch rider pulled up on his BSA 350 CC motorcycle. Tugging off his helmet and goggles, he yelled:

"Are you Jack Simmons with the Navy?"

"Yeah I am," said Jack.

"Well, sorry Sir, but your leave is cancelled. Make your way to Portsmouth right now and be there by 1600". The dispatch rider handed Jack a pass for London Transport and a one-way fare on the London and Great Southern Railway. And with that the honeymoon was over.

A long kiss to Bette, handshakes and nods to guests, with little time for sentiment. A few apologies as if it was his fault that a war was on and then Jack was gone. He boarded a red London bus and headed through the prior night's remains of the bombing raids for Waterloo Station where he boarded the 1330 train. It was not full and Jack had almost the entire carriage to himself. Down the end were three young soldiers, singing dirty songs...

something to do with Hitler and Himmler and their testicle size. Or was it how many they had between them?

Jack Simmons had met Bette sometime in September 1939, at a fete in the country near Canterbury, which is close to London. Ironically, the function included Tom Gale, whose sister, Kitty, was a good friend of Bette's. Jack had joined the navy before the war and was very slowly climbing up the promotion ladder. He had been a cobbler's apprentice after high school, where he had just scraped through graduation, but he got called up and was pleased to join the Navy, and see the world. So far all he had seen of the world was a parade ground, the south of England, and had been a bit sea sick on the few channel exercises he'd been on. He was keen to marry Bette, after a year of courting her and was glad that he was now legally married. But without her presence he felt awfully glum and lonely.

He watched the scenery go by: many bombed buildings and vehicles and even a big red bus which was just a pile of metal now, perched on top of a three storey high pile of rubble. Another pile was from mostly the remains of Stuttaford's Department Store that had been a thriving business the day before. As the train steamed on beyond the outskirts of London there was less destruction and more pleasant countryside to watch. England at its best with huge oak trees and rolling green grassy hills. And then, there between the trees, a glimpse of a mansion probably over 500 years old. He thought about Bette and what his weekend would have been like, compared to being on board a ship. He could not believe how bad his timing had been and he felt so sad.

Jack reached Portsmouth, a naval port on the south coast of England. By 1500 he was on board HMS Yacht, Rosabelle, a small vessel of 551 tons purchased by the Admiralty in 1939, for patrol services. She was well armed and her job was to hunt and destroy U-Boats. Intelligence reports had discovered there would be more than usual U-boat activity tonight, hence poor Jack's leave being cancelled.

Jack went to his on-board station immediately. He was a steward and he had to ready all the equipment and paraphernalia associated with feeding the crew. By 1600 the ship was out into the channel. At 0421, on December 11 1941, U-374, Unno von Fischel, a German U-Boat, just off the coast of Spain, on the hunt for prey, sighted HMS Rosabelle. Nobody knew the U-Boat was in the vicinity and no signal was raised. U-374 fired just one torpedo hitting HMS Rosabelle amidships, right through the dining room, into the ammunition depot. The massive flash of exploding ammunition could be seen well over the horizon.

Below the sea the crew of U-374 cheered and hugged each other. Above, all aboard the Rosabelle were lost. The timing of the attack was only discovered when U-374 herself was hit by the Royal Navy and stranded off the coast of Ireland some four months later. Many on board the German submarine were rescued and then interrogated by the Royal Navy. Only then was it discovered that among other ships sunk in an eighteen month period by U-374 that HMS Rosabelle had been one of them. Bette had received only a "missing in action" telegram from the admiralty, four days after her wedding.

Earlier, on her wedding day, at the Belgrave Hotel, Bette had to beg for her deposit back and explained the reasons why. The hotel staff sympathized and were persuaded to return her money. Then she had Jack's best man drive her back home, along with her mother, Florence, known as Florrie and her two younger sisters, Edie and Lily. It wasn't far, about two miles through the winding lanes of Kennington, near the oval cricket grounds.

Time for Bette to be angry at the war and frustrated at what she was going through. If truth be known, although she would never admit it, Bette was also embarrassed. She also was unaware that she was soon to become a widow. In fact, it was nearly four months later that she received notice from the Navy that "Able seaman J. Simmons was lost at sea and assumed deceased".

Bette had done a quick change at the Belgrave Hotel where she had left her honeymoon dress. Now, carrying her wedding dress and the rest of her belongings, she was returning home. This was the very same home she had left that very morning and neighbours would surely notice her return and start asking questions, and she was right. Edie and Lily were carrying their brides-maids dresses too, with other possessions in a small suitcase.

A group of women neighbours were in the middle of the street, gossiping, then when they saw the family returning home they started yelling across the street in a kind-hearted fashion.

"I thought you were on honeymoon," enquired one neighbor in her typical Cockney accent, dropping all the "H"'s from the beginning of words. Also dropping the

"G'"s from the end of words. This was a part of London where cockneys lived, so they all spoke the same.

"Aren't you supposed to be at some fancy hotel?" asked another.

"Wot a shame. Did something go wrong deary?" asked another lady from across the street.

"Did that sod leave you at the altar?" yelled the old biddy next door.

Even though Bette was tough and outwardly valiant she barely managed to nod then smile and rush inside the house before bursting into tears. Edie, who was the baby of the house at age nineteen now had to share a single bed with Bette. This was the very same bed she had shared with Bette for over three years but as of today had assumed was hers alone. The house was one of twelve row houses all joined together. The neighborhood was lower middle class but everyone worked and they all respected their neighbours. The war had really intensified the caring each had for one another. When they had lawns they were bright green and well cared for. Today there was no water and no lawns. Nobody on that street owned a car but some owned bicycles to get to work and back. At the corner was a pub, The Whistling Duck, where most residents used to spend many happy hours together.

The day was difficult and who knew what type of conversation one could have without tempers flaring if someone said the wrong thing? They picked at some leftover soup and tried playing a boardgame, Snakes and Ladders, but really their hearts weren't in it. They tuned in to the small wireless and listened to the 6'o'clock BBC news. It wasn't good. The allied forces had not won any battles that day. In fact most Brits at this stage of the war thought they would lose. Bombing every night and Rommel beating them in North Africa, Hitler winning everywhere, how could England survive? And few ships were arriving with supplies from America.

After the grizzly news was over nobody felt like listening to Tommy Handley, the currently fashionable comedian on the wireless. "I cannot stand that silly man" Bette's mother, Florrie, lamented, then picked up her library book, Martha's Girls, by Arlene Hughes and read the same paragraph in the book she had read five times at least. "Let's all 'ave a cuppa tea," volunteered Edie, "then we can all play I-Spy and have a good giggle, alright?" The rest mumbled, "Okay for the tea. Let's think about a game after we've had the tea".

"Better get them curtains drawn, blackout's in three minutes," Florrie said, " then we can have an early night and tomorrow I shall make all of us a nice pancake breakfast. I think I 'ave a whole lemon and a small amount of sugar lent to me by Uncle George's, girl, Pat". All of them drew down their black out curtains and retired for the night. Blackout was a law which meant no lights to shine through any house windows after sunset, which was 1800, in December. Mostly it worked but the German pilots knew where they were headed anyway, especially when the moon shone on the river Thames.

The ladies had only just laid their heads down when the air raid siren started up at about 2100. The siren slowly growled as the warden hand-cranked it and then the speed increased and that dreadful wail up and then down and on and on. The warden and his siren were on the roof of the local council office down the street from them, on Kennington Road near the oval cricket grounds. They could hear the planes coming over. They were German Dorniers and probably a hundred of them. All with that distinctive whirr as they roared over London. Using the S-bend of the river Thames as a guide, the Luftwaffe pilots split up for their arranged targets. Then, as if the day hadn't already been gloomy enough, Bette's house was struck by a direct hit. Maybe thirty bombs were dropped on Kennington Road alone, that night.

Not one house on their street survived and no human survived, except Bette. She was buried under a large table in the dining room. Bette's bed, along with the entire second floor had collapsed and with the roof bearing down on it, had pushed everything onto the ground level floor. Her mum was dead and both Edie, nineteen, and twenty-one year old Lily, were dead. Both were somewhere far from Bette in the rubble that had been their bedroom for a few hours until that damn nazi bomb hit them. Bette was buried but alive and she screamed and hoped the rescue workers she could hear up above would hear her. But apparently they did not. Seventeen hours went by. Bette became weak and frantic and lost for ideas on what to do next. One thing for sure, there was no way she could dig herself out from under that table. Fate sometimes plays an important role in people's lives and for Bette it happened in the nick of time.

She could hear the rescue workers maybe only four or five feet above and they were starting to leave. "There's no hope left, captain," yelled out one fireman. "If there's anyone down there they can't be alive. Let's pack it in and get something to eat and get our heads down. We've been here for seventeen bleedin' hours". Bette heard all this and her panic became even greater. All of a sudden a fireman lost his valuable and hard to replace fireman's boot in a gap in the rubble. He put his arm down in the hole and waved it around until he felt his lost boot. At that moment, Bette saw the hand and reached out from under the table and grabbed it. The fireman screamed and clutched his heart and yelled, "WAIT....There's someone alive down here".

Rescuers scrambled up to where he was and furiously dug and removed slabs of brick and cement and roof tiles and wooden framework. Some had bleeding hands and even though their gloves were threadbare they never stopped digging. Then they shoved aside a huge solid table and a relieved Bette crawled out from the rubble. They hauled her out with two or three firemen on each arm under her armpits and dragged the strapping Bette out into the fresh air. "Get your hands off me, they're filthy!" she cried out and then looked down at herself. She had no bleeding or bruises but was utterly filthy. Then she broke down and let it all out.

They wrapped a blanket around Bette, hiding the stains on her nightdress, placed her in an ambulance and sent her to the nearest hospital for a check-up. "Just let me out of here," cried Bette "The hospital is needed for sick people and there's nothing wrong with me".

"Yes, dearie, we know, it's just procedures alright?" hushed the nurse as she wiped the dirt off Bette's face and arms. It was only at the hospital that Bette found out the fate of her mother and two sisters. She allowed her stiff upper lip to soften and she wept uncontrollably. Then, bringing herself back to her normal "big girl for daddy" composure, she said to herself, "all right then, grow up and get on with it".

Early the next morning Bette's younger brother, George, was on a bus headed for the bombed house. He had been in Plymouth, training to go overseas, when he was granted leave to attend Bette's wedding. He had only just returned to his barracks when he was told about the bombing and his mother's and sister's deaths. He was given another twenty- four hours compassionate leave before shipping out to active duty. Of course there was rubble everywhere and George, who was born in that same bombed house on Kennington Road, had no idea where he was. He was now married and lived elsewhere with his wife, Pat, in between military training, He was now very confused and asked the bus driver, "Wot are you a doing of stopping here?"

"Well this is your street so get orf and tell 'em all down there how sorry I am," replied the driver.

George got off the bus and entered hell. There was not one house even recognizable. In fact, he did not know which direction to walk as no numbers were visible and all he could see were officials scouring the ruins for any survivors or pets or to ensure no gas or electricity was leaking. George had lived and played on this street for over twenty years but could find no landmark. Nothing he saw gave him a clue as to which rubble used to be his home.

He approached a policeman and recognized him as the regular "Copper" who had patrolled the same street for years before the war. The constable recognized George and said, "Look 'ere George, I wouldn't go any further if I was you. They're all gone and only Bette survived and she's alright, mind you, just go down to Princess Beatrix 'orspital and visit 'er there".

George was sobbing and tears started running down the constable's face too. "Yeah, I think you're right," replied George. Then he stood to attention and did a perfect royal marine salute; an about turn and marched off as quickly as he could and he never ever went back to that street again. As he left, George said to the Policeman "Don't let me near any Germans today 'cos I would be up for murder. I'd like to get my hands on one right this minute. Bastards!"

Meanwhile Bette arranged the funerals. A week later, at the cemetery near Clapham Common, which was the neighbourhood where they had lived, a small group of three mourners, Pat, her sister-in-law and Gracie, her friend, said goodbye to the three Swan ladies. George had already left for overseas duty and could not be there for that sad funeral. The war still had not taken enough and relentlessly more and more innocent Londoners were still to be fodder for the bloody Nazi bombers.

It was at the funeral that Bette decided that she wanted to contribute to the war effort and that thought led her to apply to become an ambulance driver. She went for her interview two days later. The ambulance service needed many more drivers, but there was a lot of learning to do than simply driving. When she rang the organization she was told to pick up a handbook which explained what she would have to undergo before she qualified as a driver of an official ambulance. Bette dutifully picked one up at the local office the very next day. As Bette would, she read the entire pamphlet and knew it inside out by the next day.

2

A FRESH START

Bette went to Ramsgate which is a lovely seaside resort south of London, for her "audition". She was asked to get behind the wheel of a large Ford ambulance and say nothing but drive to where the instructor told her. The instructor must have been turned down at some time in his life as a drill sergeant in the army. He yelled and cursed and frightened the hell out of Bette. She was not in the mood for his abuse and told him so.

"Listen here, my man, you need drivers and I am volunteering to be one. If this is the way you treat your candidates then I am surprised you have any. Now then I am driving back to your base and I am leaving Ramsgate and will go across to Canterbury, which was about twelve miles west of Ramsgate. When I leave I want a note from you recommending that location for me, understand? If I don't have your note in my hand I will stay here and tell everyone about your attitude." He blanched; nobody had spoken to him that way before. Bette left shortly thereafter with a glowing report from the instructor.

The next day Bette reported to Canterbury Air Raid Precautions Department, the ARP, which controlled the ambulance service. Her days were filled with learning. First Aid lessons along with how to recognize symptoms like shock, delusion and anger, and how to cope with certain patients to calm them down or restrain them. Even how to administer certain medications, although the hospitals did not like drivers doing so. A lot of instruction was devoted to how to place patients onto a stretcher, especially those with back issues.

Drivers were taught vehicle maintenance such as replacing batteries and minor tune-ups to the engine and how to fill up with fuel. After two weeks of this came the actual driving skills: two days of riding over rubble in the streets and what the vehicle would feel like cornering at high speed, skid control, reversing with mirrors only. Then a few hours of bookkeeping and learning some code words and how to communicate on the radio. Then Bette was given a certificate confirming that she was now a qualified ARP ambulance driver.

She was posted to the London docks area in January 1942. This was one of the very worst places to be during any bombing raid because the Germans concentrated so much bombing on London's dockyards. Bette was introduced to Beryl, her partner, who was senior to Bette as she had been driving for over four months. There was quite a high casualty rate for ambulance drivers and they needed to watch out for each other. The bombs started falling on the very first night Bette arrived. They had been instructed to wait at an assembly point about a mile north of the docks, and to study their maps showing the grids and sections they may be called to and to wait until they were called.

The wait was not long. The radio blared, "Base to 26," (Bette's ambulance was 26) "proceed to 113 Falmouth Crescent. Remove victims and take to Battersea Hospital." Beryl started up and they screamed through the streets to the site at up to 60 mph as the streets north of the docks were clear of any rubble that night. Upon arrival they could see at least twelve other ambulances in attendance. There were fires and steam escaping from underground pipes and policemen waving frantically for them to drive forward past the other ambulances.

"We've got some bad ones 'ere darlin'," said the constable as he stuck his head through the driver's side window. "Park over by that blue car and don't say I didn't warn you." The two got out and found three children, around age four or five, all completely limbless and one even headless.

The woman next to the children was barely alive and she was the three girls' mother. Bette and Beryl picked up the mother. They gently placed her on a stretcher and slid her into the ambulance and told the police the children were all dead and they needed other transport. Meanwhile, they raced off to the nearest hospital in Battersea, which was a suburb in middle London. The mother was screaming about leaving her kids behind "who will look after them if I die"? she yelled. Bette gave her a quick shot of morphine as she could see the woman was in danger of losing her left leg and perhaps had pain in her back. Only ten minutes later they reached the hospital. They had radioed ahead to describe the patient and nurses were on standby to remove the mother out and into the emergency room. That night, one hundred and sixty-two other patients were being attended to, mostly in the hospital's corridors because of the increasing numbers of patients.

Seven more runs were completed that night. They were on the 2000 to 0800 shift and generally the intensity was always from about 2100 until about midnight, when the German bombers usually left and relative tranquility descended.

Bette and Beryl shared a pre-fabricated home in a barracks for ambulance drivers. There were two quarters in each home each with two small bedrooms. Bette's bedroom was seven foot by nine foot with a single bed and a chest of drawers. The two shared a small bathroom with a toilet and a sink. Bath tubs were available but shared by eight houses. This arrangement generally worked out fine as one could schedule a bath in between other's working shifts. That first morning Bette got into her bed at about 0830. She was exhausted but also the adrenalin would not stop rushing through her body. Still, she soon fell fast asleep and was roused by Beryl at 1900 after almost ten hours of sleep. There was a mess hall for the sixty women who lived in the ambulance barracks, Bette and Beryl headed off to their dinner before heading out for their 2000 shift. Their meal that night was oxtail soup, salisbury steak with mushy peas and mashed potatoes, followed by a small rice pudding. All good "stick to the ribs" food to sustain them through the night. Three cups of tea later and a quick visit to the toilet and by 1930 they were gone.

London was a noisy dust bowl with roads filled with rubble from the constant bombing. They had to drive through this to get to their assembly point. Beryl was a chain-smoker and Bette could not stand the smell of smoke. About a week after becoming Beryl's partner, Bette was chatting with Laura in the mess. She was another driver who said she was upset at her partner being a heavy smoker. The two liked each other and Bette went to the manager and "schmoozed" him. "Look", she said with a twinkle in her eye "if I ever wanted to become a manager here, I suppose I would have to learn things about people, like you and decide how to arrange them. Right. What if there were four drivers and two of them smoked?"

"Oh yes," he replied, all knowing and all correct. "Now in the instance you mention, it is very obvious what to do. Keep everyone happy and put the two smokers together and the others together. That is what I would do". Bette summed it all up and said "So you don't mind if I place Beryl with a smoker which lets me join a non-smoker? I have all the names, so to be fair to you it would keep your records straight." What could he say? Bette moved in with Laura that night and Beryl got chain-smoker Amanda. Done. Everyone happy, especially Bette.

Every night was a crisis. Attending to bombed-out buildings Bette sometimes remembered visiting before the war. There was a bank or maybe that cinema and so many others just lying in ruins. One night the Carlton

Cinema was hit just a few minutes after the siren had sounded. No matter that twenty-three ambulances rushed to the scene, some only a few minutes after the first bomb fell, nobody could save the 137 cinema goers burned alive inside.

Bette remembered speaking to a middle-aged gentleman outside the cordoned-off area. The police were trying desperately to stop him running inside. "But my wife is in there, "he pleaded. "I said I would protect her for the rest of my life. I must get her out. Listen ambulance lady," he shouted at Bette, "follow me in there I know exactly where she was sitting. I only went to the lobby to get her an ice lolly." Whenever Bette mentioned that incident she would tear up. "Poor old geezer, he couldn't know that nobody inside that huge oven was alive. The only people who survived, maybe a hundred of them, were those near the back exits and in the lobby." The rest were taken away by mortuary ambulances.

One night after Bette became a lead driver, but still working with Laura, the two of them were sitting in their ambulance close to 2300. With no bombers appearing at all they decided to patrol the streets to stay awake and see if they could find something to do; a civilian accident perhaps? An hour later four Dornier Luftwaffe bombers swooped across London and dropped about forty bombs. Whether this was a new tactic by the Germans or those four bombers had gone astray, didn't matter to Bette and Laura. All they knew was from radio reports was that the small cafe near where they had been parked for most of the night had been demolished by one of the bombs.

They too would not have survived had they not moved. Fate, once again.

A few months later, toward the end of 1942, they transferred Bette further north, near Dagenham, an industrial part of Essex, not far from central London. She spent many months in that area, mostly dealing with patients who were in the military: the wounded from various parts of the world where British troops were fighting. More and more wounded were Americans, mostly air force and mostly suffering with burn injuries.

In June of 1944 she was moved again some 200 miles north to near Newcastle, on the east coast of England. Bette was getting to see a lot of English places she had never seen before. She had only been in Newcastle for a week when she was radioed to take a wounded soldier from an airfield to an army hospital. Bette was driving an old American Buick that had the back cut off and then fitted out as an ambulance. She and her new assistant, Moira, raced the fifteen miles to the airport.

When Bette went into the main building she asked, "Where should I park to load up the wounded soldier?"

"Hold on a minute," replied a man in some uniform, "he is right here. He can walk but he can't talk. I shall get him for you. You stay where you are." A few minutes later the uniformed man came around the corner helping a young Royal Marine soldier who was walking slowly with his face all bandaged up, "Here he is, Miss," announced the uniformed man. "Now son go along with that lady driver." He disengaged his arm and Bette came forward to help him outside and into the ambulance.

Bette said gently, "Come along, Sir, I will....my God! It's George".

Indeed it was her brother George, who had phoned her three days before to say he was going overseas, and he didn't know where, and if he didn't make it back to please help his wife, Pat. There he was, with a very bloody, puffy face and in extreme pain. Bette got him to the ambulance and she administered a shot of morphine. To hell with the hospitals not liking me administering medicines, Bette thought. Once the morphine started to kick in, George managed to mumble. "I was in a para- jump into France and gerry was all over the place. Our regiment marched into a small village and some bleedin' fat-arsed bastard gerry killed my captain who was patrolling next to me. I bayoneted the sod and as he fell backwards he shoved his bleedin' rifle into my mouth and smashed most of my teeth out. All the nerve ends are revealed and I need emergency surgery; actually what he said sounded like "obb my nerb eds are wevealed and I need emerhency urgeree." Apparently some Yanks in a jeep had rescued George from being captured by the Germans. The G.I.'s rushed him to an airstrip, which the allies had seized. They had a Mitchell transport plane flying over to Newcastle and they put George on it. Then some young Doctor, on board the plane, stuck a needle, filled with some pain-killer, into George's neck. George said afterwards, "I tell you whatever that stuff was the Yanks gave me was bloody wonderful. That young Doctor assured me I would never feel pain again, while I was under his care, what a bloke. I think he was about my age and I am going to suggest the Royal Marines get some of that medicine or more doctors like him".

Bette was crying with pity that her brother was in such bad shape and only twenty-six years old, but also with relief that he was going home and his injuries were not life threatening. She got him to the army hospital within thirty minutes where George was soon operated on, given some crowns and bridges, and sent home to his wife, Pat, for three weeks to recuperate.

One night Bette's vehicle broke down. She had been trained to perform regular maintenance like topping up oil, coolant, battery acid and so on. This one evening she had a flat front right, driver's side tire. She and Moira got the ambulance off to the side of the road and Bette got out the jack and the wrench and proceeded to change the wheel.

While she was crouching down and Moira was keeping a lookout for traffic on this very narrow country road, a car raced by them. Perhaps the driver had been drinking? In any event, he hit Bette a glancing blow right on her rear end and she was shot into the air and landed in some hedges sealing off the road from the field. Moira screamed and ran to help Bette.

At that very moment another ambulance drove by and screeched to a halt. That driver was a mechanic returning a newly serviced ambulance back to the depot. Between the mechanic and Moira they managed to get Bette off the hedge and into the ambulance. They left their broken down ambulance on the road. Nobody ever found the hit and run driver.

They got Bette to the hospital and she was already turning red and black bruising all up her rump and arm and she had thorns stuck in her face but she once again escaped any meaningful damage. They x-rayed her and smothered soothing lotion everywhere and let her sleep in a bed for one night. She then recuperated in her quarters for a week. Newcastle area was not as busy as London and Bette asked if she could return to the London Docks. She was well liked and she got her way. Soon she was back and once again partnered with Laura.

Ambulances were not to pick up the dead as there were special mortuary ambulances for that purpose. One evening Bette and Laura had to drive to a direct bomb strike on a double-decker bus. The bus was not recognizable. A ton of twisted metal with all the red paint burned off and thirty-three dead passengers in hundreds of pieces scattered everywhere. Bette remembered thinking about where those people were headed. What if there were young children at home wondering where their mother or father were. What if there was a disabled person waiting at home for his or her medications or dressing changes and their spouse simply never returned?

She went right into the wreck desperately searching for wallets, handbags, labels in clothing; anything to try identifying the victims. Regretfully, the bomb had done its job and the ensuing fire had destroyed everything in its range. Bette was so despondent over that particular bombing that she said it stuck with her for decades after the war. The thought of orphaned children and disabled human beings stayed with Bette forever. She used those thoughts to drive her ambitions later on in life.

Bette's career as an ambulance driver was exciting and thrilling and tiring and wonderful. She enjoyed everything about it and did not relish returning to regular civilian life when the war ended. In spite of the cruelty and sadness and the horrific scenes almost every night, Bette was glad she was contributing to the war effort, which she most certainly was.

Not that she ever needed more confidence than she already had, but the way she felt and her increased energized poise certainly contributed to her ability to survive and get things done whenever she was confronted with challenges the rest of her life.

The war seemed less extreme at home, at least the bombing was less frequent and less intense. However, every now and then the Germans would have a push on to demoralize the British civilians and there would be a huge raid. These raids were much like the intensity of the Blitz that occurred at the beginning of the war. London was a dark, dusty and gloomy place to be and yet carried on as if this was the normal way of life. Bette was still a very busy driver.

3

TOM'S FIRST ACTION

Tom Gale was a Rifleman in the King's Rifle Corp. He was about 5 ft. 10 inches and very slim. He had a devil-ish grin and was never sure about what he wanted to do when he grew up. He started wood-joining and cabinet making but he was bored, so he signed up for the regular Army in 1933. His first posting was to the Winchester Depot which is about seventy five miles south-east of London. After training in 1934, he was posted to the First Battalion in Gosport, a naval port located on the south coast. When war broke out he found himself at Dorset Blandford, a town of less than 12,000 people on the River Stour in Dorset.

Because Winston Churchill was going on about being ready and able to attack and penetrate France, Army HQ had a great idea to test what an invasion of Europe would be like. If they could do it, maybe Hitler could do it too. After all France was not much more than twenty-two miles away. Special squads were set up to cover as many contingencies as army HQ could anticipate.

Then Dunkirk materialized and thousands of allied soldiers, mostly British, were trapped on a beach in France while being attacked by a huge German force. If there was any way to save them Churchill would do it. It was then that the military put into play its reserve units, like the one Tom was in, especially created to cause diversionary tactics and to split the enemies' forces.

At 1400, on Tuesday, May 21, 1940, 3,000 men drove through the night to Dover and boarded two troop-carrying ships that were all steamed up and able to depart immediately. The ships actually had to leave some troops behind. Even standing up on the open decks there was no room for even one more soldier. They arrived at Calais at 1600 on May 22nd. The sailing itself was fraught with danger as U-Boats patrolled the English Channel and were extremely successful at sinking British ships. But they made their destination safely. The plan was to get on the beaches of Calais and kill or capture every German they found. But the real plan was to help the poor sods in Dunkirk by getting a large portion of the German army to leave Dunkirk and come up to defend Calais. This would at least give the Dunkirk troops an opportunity to fight back and get off the beach back to England.

Of course there are plans and then there is reality. The men would get off the ships and get on to the beaches, then see how far they could get inland before… well, before what? It is doubtful that the brass in HQ had gone beyond thinking about getting off the ships, let alone getting off the beaches. But the job had to be done and nobody had any experience in those matters. At the planned time 3,000 very brave men hit the beaches. There were about 1,000 French already in Calais, helping the British to defend themselves against an increasingly more powerful German army as they arrived from Dunkirk. A total of 4000 fighting the most vicious battle ever.

They got off the ships but the water was much deeper than they were told it would be. The troops had been told the sea would be about a foot deep but it was about four feet. Some men tried swimming while others were in canvas boats and others were in a new form of landing craft. Some were inside armoured vehicles and had powerful Vickers mounted machine guns. Any German hit by a Vickers would be unlikely to survive if only someone knew where to aim. It was bedlam as it was pitch black. Everyone knew they had to get onto the beach then get to the cliff on the other side. Many died right there in the sea, or two or three feet onto the beach. Others died without moving a foot or even getting a foot wet.

Frankly, the mission was doomed, and everyone knew it, but their mission was too important and they were ordered to fight to the last man. The longer they could keep large numbers of Germans in Calais, the better chance the 150,000 could get out of Dunkirk. They were met by a hail of bullets mortars and rifle fire. Over 20,000 German troops were waiting for them all armed with the rapid firing Mauser MG 42, a gun so fast it seemed as if a hundred thousand German troops were firing at them. Two German divisions had been pulled from the fight against the British Expeditionary Force now struggling to get out of Dunkirk. And these Germans were already hardened and battle trained. No time to think about what happened just best to move and find a safe place, out of the way of that never ending noise of bullets and screams.

In military terms, when your outfit has over 30% casualties, which means dead, prisoners of war and injured, one cannot be expected to continue with such high losses and expect to win. This is not to say that the "Boffins" in HQ were expected to know everything no matter how well trained or even experienced they were. They were only human with a job to do but it was a war and someone had to plan for events that were not included in any training courses. It was almost impossible to plan ahead when nothing like the plan has ever been done before. With modern warfare and equipment, history was of little use in the planning. Army HQ had no doubt researched the Spanish Armada and the various invasions by the Greeks and the Romans. With memories of World War I attempts also being on their minds and so on but what they learned could not have possibly been much use at all in 1940.

The modern part of the town, St-Pierre, lies to the south and south-east. In the centre of the old town in the Place d'Armes stands the Hôtel-de-ville along with the town hall and police offices. This invasion was during the Dunkirk operation and the Germans were all up and down that French coast and occupied Calais. It was not going to be easy for the allies to win over a permanent force. The Germans were hiding in the port piers and docks as well as snipers in the third and fourth floors of the few buildings with more than one floor. Calais had been bombed by allies and the Axis forces and there wasn't much left standing. The old part of the town, Calais proper (known as Calais-Nord), is situated on an artificial island surrounded by canals and harbours.

Each British soldier had a kit on his back weighing over forty pounds. Add to that the extra weight of the seawater soaking through their battledress uniforms and a heavy Enfield rifle with five pouches of 303 ammunition strapped to the belt. Just putting one foot in front of the other was an enormous task and running was almost superhuman. Adrenaline did help. Tom remembered his mate, Lance Corporal Digby Evans, was puffing and out of breath as they trudged, up to their buttocks in the sea. Digby yelled, "Bloody 'ell, where are they shooting fr..." then his head burst open as he fell down dead.

Tom hesitated, looked down at his mate wondering if he could help then heard a bullet crack past his head. Any thought of stopping ended at that very moment. He ripped off his back pack and grabbed his rifle to hold it high and out of the waves and somehow made it ashore. Now for the base of those shallow cliffs, where the Germans couldn't point down at that angle. He could make those forty or fifty steps, he thought.

Tom stood terrified at 1900 with hundreds of his mates lying on the beach covered in blood and sand and dead and dying. He had a rifle and would have aimed and shot at every German there if only he knew where they were. Tom was halfway to the relative safety of the shallow trench nature had built at the base of the cliff. It was really more like a thirty foot high sand-dune than a cliff. He ducked behind an ambulance but bullets were flying from all directions. Finally he ran to a small dune and managed to dig down in enough sand to stay out of the angle of fire. The battle for Calais lasted four days until May 25th. The Luftwaffe showered the troops with pamphlets pleading with them to surrender or be killed. The longer they fought, the more chance the British Expeditionary Force (BEF) could escape Dunkirk. But there would be no surrender.

On the last day of fighting very few British troops were able to fight anymore. Tom had not slept for two nights and was now once again trying to stave off sleep. Amidst bullets cracking past him he curled up in a small trench. This time he had found a Bren gun with maybe 4,000 rounds of ammunition. He was pointing up the cliff, and at the German's position. His Bren was no match for the Germans Mauser but it was a hell-of-a-lot better than his Enfield rifle. Tom was also a pretty good marksman, so he was getting in some great shots. But he wanted to get out of that trench and was planning his next move when a Warrant Officer, or as Tom called him. "The bloke wots in charge of the beach during the war," came jumping into the shallow fox hole alongside Tom.

He shouted into Tom's ear, "Gale can you drive?"

Tom had a driving lesson in 1938. He tried to be truthful "Well yes I have had driv….".

The W.O. cut him off, "Good, then take that bleedin' ambulance and get it to our medic. He's about five miles down the road at a farmhouse with a platoon of blokes all wounded. They need those medical supplies in there or most will die".

"Okay, anything is better than sitting 'ere chatting with you," said Tom, as he scrambled over to the ambulance, got behind the wheel, and after a few false starts, and crashing of gears, managed to get off the beach . It was 1100 hours.

The going was not easy. He drove through a gauntlet of German bullets. "The bleedin' ambulance body was like sheet metal lace," he said afterwards. "Bullets hit everything but the engine and me." He raced along the winding road at full speed with the Austin's six cylinder 70 horsepower engine screaming for mercy as he had it in third gear all the way. At best he reached maybe forty miles an hour and now mortar shells were exploding in front and alongside him.

After what seemed like half a day, but in reality was less than twenty minutes, Tom found the only house in sight, a small farmer's cottage filled with allied soldiers. A few burned out or broken down army vehicles were scattered around and Tom swerved around them and drove into the pasture. He managed to stop by driving into the hedge as all brakes had been shot out and did not work. The engine knocked itself out and suddenly it was deathly quiet.

The medic was a young Captain. He had on a battle-dress jacket that was soaked in blood and mud. He and two or three of the least wounded soldiers came hobbling out and helped Tom empty the ambulance. Bandages, morphine, blankets and a crude surgical kit. Inside the house was chaos. Screaming and moaning men, with limbs shattered or lost and entrails being held in place by trousers and blankets and hands. Morphine syringes were found and administered to just about everyone. That quietened down most men. One Regimental Sergeant Major had his left foot blown off. "My effing foot is back on the beach with my boot…what a bleedin' waste of polish. I 'ope it doesn't get sunburned out there all day". The morphine was working on him and his attempt at black humour did get a murmur of chuckles from some of the men. Typical of an RSM to get the men to stop thinking about their wounds and try to be positive. Several men smiled as the Morphine entered their blood stream and then they simply rolled over and died. Triage ensued and only those whom the Captain thought had a chance were attended to. Indeed they might now have a chance if only they could be taken to a hospital.

At 1600 hours a trail of dust could be seen getting closer to the farmhouse. Four German half-tracks and a Mercedes convertible stuffed with well-fed officers and a young bespectacled fresh-faced NCO driver came into view. The driver looked scared and flushed. Most probably he had only just recently been promoted from his Hitler Youth Brigade. The Germans arrived in a cloud of dust and as they took off their caps and goggles their faces had an outline of dust with white patches around their eyes. They tried to get rid of the dust by smacking themselves with their caps but all they accomplished really was to simply redistribute it.

The leader of the group in his baggy jodhpurs and once shiny high boots marched a few paces to the front of the house and stopped as the British Captain emerged.

Four German regulars cocked their rifles and pointed them at the Captain. "That is alright, men," shouted the German officer, "lower your weapons."

The medic went out and greeted them civilly, wiping a bloodied bandage across his brow. He saluted and said, "I am Captain Harrison of The Kent Rifles, Medical Corp. I haven't checked but I believe there are no weapons here and if there were there are only two of us who could even use them. I trust somebody here speaks English as I don't speak a word of German and I must get back inside to treat my men. Whatever you have to say you had better make it quick."

"I am Loitenaant Klaus Hettering of the 25 Brigade. I am sorry to meet you under these circumstances. You English amuse me because you never believe you should learn other languages. I learn my English is because I am student from Cambridge from 1932 to 1936. Anything you wish to say to me I understand (saying it like "oon-terschtend) extremely good. we are not here to kill wounded people and we simply want to get you all to a hospital. My men will help load the wounded onto our vehicles and you may go with them. The other soldier who is not injured his name please. He will go with us to a POW camp". The German typically found it difficult to say any words beginning with "TH" , they sounded like "Z". Any words beginning with a "W" sounded like a "V".

Tom Gale joined twenty other allied soldiers who were already on the back of a five ton German truck and they headed off to some unknown destination. As they bounced along in the cool breeze of the evening two machine gun toting guards at the back of the canvas covered truck smoked and chatted to each other and watched over the POW's.

Somewhere along the line every man there must have been thinking how lucky they were and how badly off nearly 4000 of their comrades had been, because they were likely all dead. Tom counted twenty-one in the truck and fourteen injured now going to a hospital some-where. Pretty damn bad odds when, as it was discovered after, it appeared less than 10% of the entire force were alive. In the end, only thirty-five escaped and only two of them, a medic and Tom, were unscathed. Nobody knows how many of the remaining 4000 survived. It has been assumed there were hardly any.

After a few hours, driving in absolute silence except for an occasional cough or sob now and then, soldiers being soldiers, shook off the gloom and started introduc-ing themselves and finding out where they had been caught and other details. One scruffy short soldier said, "'Hello my name is Gordon Jones. I am a small arms instructor. I was on the beach when I saw a gap. I ran for the gap and nearly got run over by one of our bloody ambulances. Stupid driver."

"here, let's have less of the 'stupid'," moaned Tom, "that was me driving and I remember you dashing out from behind the hedges in front of me. It is a good job I swerved. I am Tom Gale, pleased to meet you." And with a smile and outstretched arms, they shook hands.

Another man with a clean, pale face and oh-so-young looking, piped up. "Look chaps I am a second lieutenant and I speak fluent German. So anytime I can translate for any of you let me know. But don't let on to gerry as we might find it to our advantage to know what they are saying without them knowing we know. Got it? By the way, Hartley Cunningham's the name."

Then a booming voice from the back of the truck yelled out, "I'm a bleedin Sergeant and I spent four years in India. I can speak Hindustani fluently, but don't let gerry know, as we could 'ave an advantage. Peter Piper's my name." Giggles all around.

"Anyone got any money on them?" asked a lance corporal with shiny Brylcreemed hair combed straight back. He looked about age fifty while most of the others were probably in a twenty to thirty-five age range. "I am a betting man and I am willing to bet a Pound that one of the next three Germans, including these two guards with us, is named Hans. Anyone willing to put up a bet? Oh yes…mmm, sorry my name is Freddy Markham. Pleased to know you all.".

"I need a piss," yelled a fresh-faced, red-headed scruffy bloke from the front. "Ask the driver to stop," he yelled at one of the German guards, "ve all vant to pee" he said in his best mocking German-English. "Ya, ya, ve too,"replied the guard in his best broken English. "Pee shtoppin soon". He pointed to his wrist watch and indicated a time. They had been driving for nearly five hours. It was now nearly 2000. Then, some twenty-five minutes later they stopped, along with a smaller truck that had been following them. They were all taken off the vehicle for a pee break.

Tom explained, "No matter how much you need a whiz, when you 'ave to stand in front of a bloody enemy soldier pointing a Mauser MG42 at you the urge leaves you and then you feel like having a crap instead. But you get over it and then you feel a bit better."

Many of them took a moment to run on the spot and do a little jig to loosen up and stretch their legs. Then the Germans handed to each man a chunk of pumpernickel bread with about four ounces of cold, fatty roast pork. Everyone passed around a tin mug filled with cold water from a barrel on the half-track. Nobody was willing to bet as to which act gave them the most relief: the wee in the woods or eating that pork sandwich? The pork was overcooked and had no spicing but it was nutritious and they gobbled it down. Nearly twenty-four hours had gone by and nobody had eaten a thing. Perhaps fifteen minutes later the guards yelled "Raus," and everyone had to scurry back onto the truck. One of the German guards tossed a pack of twenty cigarettes and a box of matches into the group of POW's. He shouted, "Enjoy, Englanders, you have a long trip ahead of you."

One of the British soldiers grabbed the smokes and passed them around; even some non-smokers lit up. They tasted like used toilet paper dried up and shredded. If there was tobacco it was well disguised. The drive was tedious, maybe 30 KM an hour. The roads were awful as nobody was maintaining them and tank tracks had sunk into the mud days before and the sun had dried the ruts out since. Just one kilometer after another of rock hard ruts. Add awful suspension on the truck and the discomfort was terrible. This is what war is all about. Yes, there is killing and noise and planes and ships and shooting and death, but also no daily newspaper, no garbage pick-up, no decent food and few decent roads. Plus foreigners trying to live where you want to live and stop you living like you wish.

Each man was hanging on for dear life. The canvas roof of the German truck had straps hanging down and most had them wrapped around an arm. "'Ere, do you think gerry knew the French roads were going to be like this? Is that why they put these bleedin' straps on?" asked one soldier. "I don't know but I wouldn't come out for a bloody Sunday drive if I lived here. My tea kettle would be arse over tit by now," somebody yelled out.

About four hours later, sometime around 0200, they reached a dock filled with smelly ships offloading war materials consisting of mostly, tanks, trucks, field artillery and such. It seemed to these POW's that Germany had a lot of "stuff" and England was doomed. The equipment England had was rubbish by comparison to what the Germans were offloading. They discovered they were in Dieppe. They zig-zagged around concrete pyramids barriers and finally stopped outside a barbed wire gate.

Two German officers came out of a hut behind the barbed wire, and started talking near the truck. They were asking themselves why POW's had to go by boat to Germany when a train could take them to Strasbourg just as easily. The more senior ranking officer said he was informed by the "Brass" that too many trains had been attacked by partisans, who had been tipped off that POW's were on board. Too many incidents had wrecked tracks and rolling stock and each incident drained away manpower from the front line. He explained, "We already have a ship leaving for Emden, and the British are too afraid of our U-Boats and the Luftwaffe in the area, so it's a simple solution." The young fluent-in-German POW translated it all in a whispered voice.

"Maybe we outnumber the crew and we can set them orf on a lifeboat, like Cap'n Bligh and we can sail back to Blighty," piped up Peter Piper.

"Last chance to make some money," said Freddy Markham. "Anyone want to bet ten shillings?"

"Oh go on," sighed Gordon Jones, "anything to keep you quiet about your silly bet. Here, who will hold the money? Here's a quid."

"Right, yells Freddy. Tom, here is my quid grab that one out of his hand and here we go." Freddy leaned back out of the back flap of the truck, and yelled, "Hans." The sailor at the gate replied. "Yawohl". Twenty-one POW's begin howling with laughter and holding on to each other for support. Freddy snatched the two quid out of Tom's hand and said "Thanks, Gordo, sorry to take your money, but a fact is a fact and it was worth the laugh, were'nt it?"

"British." shouted one guard "Everyone off the vehicle and stand in two lines in front of this gate. "Stretching and yawning and as slow as they could be, just to annoy the Germans, the men got off the truck.. In some manner they lined up in three lines; hands in pockets and shuffling feet.

"Who is the senior man here?" asked one of the senior German officers.

"I suppose that's me," replied second Lieutenant Hartley Cunningham. "Vell, you are in charge of zis group and you vil be responsible if they do anything wrong, understand?" "Oh boy, actually in charge? This is the very first time I have ever been in charge of anything. I shall do my best. Alright Englanders?" Cunningham mocked.

"March in single lines to ze gangway. Halt when you get zere." Commanded the German officer. Like 10 year old schoolboys, giggling and hands in pockets, the twenty-one POW's, shuffled along, as if they were in a chain-gang. Then, with about fifty yards remaining to march, they all purposely did so, with left arms swinging with left legs, all copying each other. Then they were marched up the gangway of the 280 foot, 6,500 ton Tanganyika, and were met by sailors who frisked them and gave each "Englander" a sweater, a towel and a bar of soap and then directed them down below, to a large room with cots and told to argue among themselves as to who slept where.

4

TWO QUICK BOAT RIDES

By then it was nearly 0400 and they were all dog tired. The room was small and smelled of diesel fuel and cigarette smoke. Most men simply fell onto a bed and were asleep within seconds. Some had to visit the head and brush their teeth with the awful toothpaste and brush they got from the Germans, but it did the job. Pink and shiny with clean teeth, they too crashed onto the bed and slept within seconds. In spite of the smell and in spite of the noise and the fear of the future the men all slept quite soundly for seven or eight hours. Tom remembers: "gerry never came around and woke us up, and if they had some sort of Reveille we never heard it. At least I didn't, I suppose they figured to let sleeping dogs lie? Why not, if we was awake we'd only want to go to the loo and 'ave breakfast and all that.".

But, without any fanfare the Germans brought them in some very fresh pumpernickel bread, still warm, along with hard-boiled eggs, sliced cold cooked bratwurst and cheese, along with big tin mugs of coffee. Tom muttered, "Eh Gerry don't you 'ave any fried bread and baked beans like what the Geneva convention says? POW's must be fed the same food as what they're used to at home."

Well that statement went over like a lead balloon to the one German sailor bringing in the food who spoke a little English, "Englander you better shut your mouth. This is a welcome for you and tomorrow you will eat the same shit as we get on board this vessel, understand? Today Captain Ardendorff has given up rations from his own supply to welcome you on board and he will be very upset at your attitude." It was early days yet and the two enemies really didn't know how to treat each other. Reality and hatred hadn't quite yet begun. It would start very soon.

By then the British POW's had finished ablutions and breakfast and were looking for things to do to pass the time. It was now close to 1000 hours and there were no books or decks of cards and no portholes. All they had was just a few tables in the small cafeteria. As the ship lurched up and down in heavy eight to nine foot swells, they hung on to their seats, fought the urge to vomit and simply sat around chatting. For most, this was their first time in battle and the first time they had heard bullets crack near their faces as they whizzed by. It was the first time any of them had seen so much carnage. Their friends and mates mown down with bone sticking out of flesh and limbs and eyes lying around for the crows to peck at when the bullets stopped. Then there were the cries for help and a stench that would get worse as each day passed. Much of the conversation among the POW's was about war, death and blood. It had not been what they had expected.

Around 1300, off the coast from Bruges, there began a commotion of sirens, bells, yelling and a lot of Germans running hither and yon. "Englanders stay where you are" yelled a smart looking German officer decked out with scrambled egg on the peak of his cap. "We are under attack".

At that moment an almighty noise smashed into the ship and acrid smoke filled the room as everyone was thrown off their feet. "Help, we are sinking and Englanders save your own lives...abandon ship" yelled someone. Everyone jumped to their feet, ran on to the deck, shoving anyone hindering their flight, and jumping into the horrible greasy dirty sea.

"The sea seemed to be only three or four feet from the deck railing as the gerry ship sank beneath that sea," said Tom, "I raised my leg over the top rail and jumped. I wasn't scared or nuffing like that, I just wished I didn't 'ave to do it. The bleedin' water was covered in oil and filled with Germans and us English blokes alike, all screaming and swallowing water and oil and trying to stay afloat."

It seemed like three minutes but it was more like forty when the German vessel Tanganyika slipped beneath the waves and disappeared forever. "For her ze war was over," smirked Tom, as he recalled that dreadful moment. Only then did they see the Royal Navy Destroyer, HMS Tynedale, loom up beside them. She had rope ladders and netting flung over the side and a sailor with a bullhorn yelling at them from a lower deck. "Make your way to the side of the ship and climb up the ropes to safety. Watch the swells and time yourselves so you get a grip and do not start climbing until you feel steady. Take your time and hold on tight. We will help you get aboard as you reach the top".

The oil floating on the water was at least a foot deep and was becoming thick as treacle as it cooled, making clothing heavier by the second. Gasping for air and trying to discard heavy jackets while swimming toward the destroyer was just too much for some as they were not fit enough to continue. Many men simply stopped and sighed and were gone. Some waved goodbye and some even smiled, but nonetheless, they went. They slipped under the waves and joined the German ship that by then had likely settled on the ocean floor, some eighty feet below.

The rope ladder was made of the same thickness rope used to tie up the ship at dock, maybe three inches thick and woven into squares of twelve inches. In practices about twenty sailors at a time could be on the ropes. In this case there were about fifty German sailors and former POW's alike scrambling to hold on to the ropes strung over the heaving ship. The rope itself seemed about two feet thick. With greasy and freezing cold hands ("similar to my Arthritis now," said Tom, as we discussed this event) and with blurred vision due to the oil and diesel fuel the men inched their way up the ladders. Life jackets and ropes were being tossed over the side as well and some thirty men were being hauled up with Life Jackets under their armpits. It was bedlam with yelling and screaming: "naaah don't put it on that way, under your arms you stupid kraut. Don't look down, look up. Look at where you want to be not where you've been." Screamed one British sailor, from the deck of his ship.

Another Royal Navy sailor yelled, "Did you swap uniforms with a kraut? Can you understand English? Put yer bloody arms and head through the ring and tuck it under yer arms." Under yer arms I said. If it stays where you have it now you'll get the rope under your throat. Jesus bloody Christ do you want to hang yourself?" There were no replies from the poor sods in the water, who were struggling to hear the orders being shouted at them. They were pewking up oil, water, diesel fuel and yesterday's pork. They winced at the pain of the lifebelts under their armpits. Still, in spite of the noise and panic, no allied former POW's drowned. But the Germans were now POW's and some of them had. According to Captain Ardendorff, twelve German sailors were unaccounted for.

Even though their rescuer was just a destroyer, Tom later learned it was only 3500 tons, which is quite smallish in a fleet of naval warships, but it seemed enormous as they fought their way to the ropes. The sides of the ship seemed a hundred foot high, but in reality, were only 11 feet. Finally, after fifty horrific minutes everyone was on board Tynedale. Thirty or so British Tynedale sailors stood at the top of the rope ladders and reached down to heave the poor wretched men on board. They had hot water and solvent and good old carbolic soap and rinsed everyone as clean as possible. Then they wrapped everyone in blankets and led them inside the ship out of the now fiercely gusting winds. Now the tables were turned and the Germans were now POW's although nobody felt like there was any difference. Nobody had been mistreated by the Germans and now they were being treated accordingly. The Germans were all locked into the forward cafeteria and given bedding, felt mattresses, and hot tea and sandwiches of roasted chicken on white buns.

The British soldiers were put into a large meeting room toward midships and given the same as the Germans got. HMS Tynedale turned north-west and headed for Dover, just about four hours distant. Remarkably, there were few injuries among the rescued men. Some had bad lacerations; two had broken legs, but other than bruising and lungs that needed cleaning out from the inhalation of smoke and ingestion of oil and fuel, they were all in fair condition.

Of course there was sobbing and coughing as everyone tried to regain posture and composure while spitting out all that poison they had ingested. Tom recalls, "Nobody, whatever their lot in life, would want to be in a sinking and rescue operation like that one. It was pure hell".

HMS Tynedale's Captain Westlake, a dapper short man, was pleased with his new position as a host to some brave temporary guests. He marched into the large room where he introduced himself and then, hands behind his back, rocking on the balls of his feet, he spoke to the Germans. "You will be met in England by a special department group who handle, POW's, of which we have many," beamed Westlake. "You know, you Germans should think yourselves extremely lucky.

You are not faring well in this war and you now get to sit it out in the beautiful south of England, in Somerset, where cider apples and dairy cream are all over the show. If you behave, you might be allowed to have some. "He flashed a toothy smile, "Soon you will be playing cricket and enjoying our renowned British hospitality while I and my men have to carry on working to get this war over with. I doubt any of you will even bother trying to escape. Comparatively speaking you are far better off just to enjoy the rest and wait out the war. So, consider yourself lucky you are on my ship and behave yourselves and share what we can give you. Any bloody nonsense, however, and I shall have your guts for garters. Alright?" (The German officer could not translate that last quip from Westlake so he said "he will be very very cross". With a salute and an about-turn, Westlake left the Germans to give his speech to the rescued British Army.

The British were sitting at attention in the room assigned to them when Captain Westlake marched in. Westlake was delighted that he had something important to do. He surely must have had in his files a written speech for every possible situation that could ever possibly arise in the future. Winston Churchill had once said: "Impromptu speeches are not worth the paper they are written on." Westlake took his cue from Churchill and had loads of "impromptu" speeches ready and waiting. "Good afternoon, chaps," he said, in a Terry Thomas-style voice. "I am so pleased to be your host today even though it will only be for a few hours more. When we get to "Jolly Old you will be taken to an aircraft hangar at

Dover airport, where special branch agents will debrief each of you privately.

You will receive fresh uniforms and then given tickets for various means of transport to get yourselves back to wherever you will be instructed to go. Alright? England is winning this war because of men like you and until it is all over I expect the army will want to have you back fighting for them. So rest up and enjoy what we have for you to eat and drink, and may God bless you all." Westlake saluted the men and briskly marched out back to his duties on the bridge.

Tomorrow arrived quickly. A cloudy sky with drizzle and, well, it was England. Everyone voted to have bangers and mash for breakfast with baked beans, of course. They were well sated by the time the Germans left. Nobody waved farewell to the Germans as they were marched off to a few army vehicles parked on the dock-side. "Cor, look at that lot," exclaimed Tom. "They get chauffeured transport at the dock and we get to walk a bleedin' mile to the train station."

5

TOM'S NEW ASSIGNMENT

After a forty-five minute train ride Tom arrived at the Barracks in Gosport. His Adjutant had sent word requesting him to check in with him ASAP. "Look Gale," he said, "I know you've had a bit of a rough time so I want you to rest up for a day and report back to me tomorrow at 1700. If you have anyone to tell, then tell them that as of tomorrow, you will be away for at least a year, alright?" "A whole day off Sir, how kind. What would I have to do to get two days off?" snipped Tom.

Tom went to a couple of civvy pubs as he did not have anyone to see and nowhere to go in that area. He consumed a few small libations before getting into a card game at some geezer's house and thankfully finding a sofa in the geezer's lounge, where he crashed for the night and had a good ten hours sleep. "Bloody 'ell," moaned Tom "for what I lost in that card game I could have had a room at the Ritz Hotel along with a slap-up meal and even my uniform cleaned and pressed.

As it is I have a sore back from that bloody sofa and the steak and kidney pie and chips along with the cockles and whelks has me insides all churned up. Not to mention me creased uniform. I will never drink cider again."

Tom thanked his host who had absolutely no idea who he was. Tom never mentioned the sofa or his back or indeed, the dinner, but on the way to see the Adjutant he did jump off the bus outside a Boot's Chemists and bought a tin of Andrews Liver Salts. He arrived at the barracks at 1600 and went into the canteen where he poured about a quarter of the liver salts into a beer mug of water and gurgled it down. Then he belched every few seconds until he felt relief. Then sort of hobbled across the pathway to the quonsat hut that was HQ and where all the files were kept. A perfect spot to hide an Adjutant.

"Oh I see you there Gale. You are a bit early but I am free so come in out of the wet and hang your battle-dress on that hanger above the electric heater. It may iron itself out of the bloody awful condition it's in. I have asked QM stores to get you a new kit and that bag over there contains three each, singlets, underpants, khaki longs and khaki shorts. There's also three Safari type jackets which are new to you. I shall explain later. Now, please note there are no boots, just six pairs of thin cotton khaki socks, a pair of plimsolls and a pair of dress black shoes.

You'll have a beret and your Rank will now be Corporal. Your pay will be increased by three shillings a month and I don't want you spending it all at once. Got that?"

Naturally Tom was curious about the summer uniform and no boots, but before he could ask the Adjutant continued with his tone dripping with sarcasm. "See that Wellington Bomber parked out there Gale? Well at 2200 you will be on it and swanning off to Africa. I know you are a very good driver. Nothing escapes us adjutants, Gale. We took note of your very brave ambulance escapade in Calais. We got all the details from the Warrant Officer who gave you the ambulance job. He managed to get off that beach and found a way out with a French farmer's family and then onto a small boat. He was picked up by our navy and he just arrived here, a day before you. An admirable job Gale, good for you. So we, well I, have come up with a thank you by giving you a very cushy, but extremely important job.

You will be a chauffeur for a VIP as he entertains the troops in North Africa. That VIP is David Niven, the English actor who now is living in America. Heard of him, Gale? He is also a Colonel in the British Armed Forces and has volunteered to help with the morale of our chaps fighting against Rommel in Africa. God knows they need their spirits boosted. Any questions Gale?"

In fact, Niven was involved with intelligence and also the BBC with entertainment for the troops. His visit to Africa was a bit more than telling funny stories to the troops, although very little is known about these exploits.

At 2140 Tom climbed up the ladder, under the belly of the Wellington bomber, with jibes and good fellow teasing from the six man crew, some of whom happened to be from Tom's own home town and one was Canadian, who was born in Algeria but left for Canada at age two. Typically, the RAF HQ had determined that he might help in the "language area" in North Africa (Of course, and why not?).

The journey would take them straight down to the coast of Spain and then cut across down to Gibraltar, then further to Algiers. They had an extra tank of fuel in the empty bomb bay and with lots of zigging and zagging, the distance would be about 1600 miles with an estimated eight hours flight time.

So, with someone else was at the controls, flying that noisy beast, it was sleep or play cards, or read. Tom did all three, but at different times. Well, until near the end when he did all at one time: five cards fanned out in his hand, the newspaper open on his chest, he fell dead asleep from the stress of it all. The flight continued without incident and the weather was okay and gerry was nowhere to be seen. At 0800 the plane circled and landed at Algiers airport. Various British officers marched from the terminal building and up to the plane to seek out someone or something on board. An adjutant was looking for Tom.

6

FAST LEARNING CURVE

"You Gale?" asked the smooth-skinned red-haired man. "Come with me and hop to it lad. Let's get out of this sun, Left, left, left right left, c'mon get a move on. Now this here motorcar is a Humber super snipe and only has 3,000 miles on the clock. Better than any bloody American car. I know you'll take care of it 'cos I'll have your balls for pudding if you don't. Do you understood, Gale?"

"Ooh yes, Adjutant," replied Tom sarcastically.

"I'll drive so you can get the feel of the place. These bleedin' Algerian wallahs drive on the wrong side of the road in the first place. Then they disobey the few rules the country has as they all rush to say prayers which they need to make them better drivers, I believe. Now, funnily enough, they seem to have learned how to control a camel, so it's not that they're stupid, just useless with anything mechanical. Are you taking this all in, Gale?"

Tom stared mostly at the gear lever to determine which direction was first then second and, quite importantly, which way was reverse. He seldom looked up to see the eleven lanes of traffic all fighting to drive in the two lanes that were available.

"For Pete's sake, Gale, never run over a bloody camel. Forget the Germans. Kill one of these blokes' camels and they will start a holy war which will last until they have your lifetime pay cheque, your first born and your missus, in any order. I have been here for six months and I am now an official alcoholic, and I never touched a drop before I was transferred here. I was much happier marching to the tune of the RSM at training school, than living among this lot. Still, keep yer head down and yer nose clean and your short visit here may be ticketyboo. Just don't go sniffing that barmaid's apron too often and you'll make it.

Now then, see this roundabout and see that villa on the opposite side? That's where his nibs has his temporary quarters, that Niven chappy. You are going to ring his doorbell and introduce yourself and ask where you can park this car. You belong to 'im now so whatever he says is what you do. I shall be leaving you now. My office is a mile away and a good ten minute march which gives me a chance to clear my head. Here we are. Enough handholding. Goodbye Gale. Drop by if you have any issues. Ta Ta."

Tom was out of his element; he was starting to miss the company of that Adjutant. He would have even welcomed a day on the parade ground with the company Sergeant Major rather than knock on the door of this

VIP. He often thought he would have made a great door-to-door Encyclopedia salesman when he was de-mobbed. He would now have to reconsider his career options. Perhaps lion taming or tight-rope walking, anything would be less stressful than what he was doing now.

He was now at the door and trembling. Even gerry hadn't affected him as much in the heat of battle. Tom knew exactly what was going to happen. Some smart-arsed butler in starched dress army bombay khaki bloomers would open the door and snootily, and most reluctantly, allow him in. Then he would have to wait at attention in the vestibule while Niven would saunter in with his uniform all askew and interview him as if he were some new houseboy.

The bell went and the door flew open. David Niven was standing there soaking wet, with a bath towel around him and moth-eaten wooly slippers on. Niven grinned and put out his arm around Tom's shoulder. "Come in old boy, you must be my driver, Tom? Call me David. You look like you could drown a cold beer. Look I'm just having one, so sit down over here and let's get to know each other. Nowhere to drive me for a day or two so you can relax. I shall get your kit from your car and Enrique can park it and get your room ready. By the way, I am a Colonel and you belong to me, so to speak, so no one can push you around except me. If anyone starts with you then call me and we shall end that nonsense right away. I am not the pushing-around type so you shall have a fine time. Let's enjoy each other. Enrique bring me my dressing gown.

Look here, it's almost lunch time. Would you care for some roast chicken and a salad, that's what they are whipping up for me. Damn fine cooks you know, trained by the French. So? Yes? Or an omelet perhaps? I am guessing you do not fancy a corned beef sandwich, hmmm? Okay, chicken it shall be." Then a servant wearing a red fez and typical Arab clothing carried four very large ice cold Heinekin beers on a silver tray into the posh living room. He also carried David's terry cloth gown over his arm.

Tom and David commenced their lovely relationship, which ended only when David died in 1983, having sent a card to Tom just a few months prior. They had corresponded every year since the end of the war. Two lovely pen pals who thought the world of each other. All day long the two men talked about England from Tom's point of view first then David's stories about early days in England compared to his finer lifestyle in New York and Hollywood. Tom was from another world, from a quite poor background whereas David was from an upper middle class family in England. Then of course he was in Hollywood, earning in a month what Tom might not earn in a decade. Never once did David try to impress Tom. David Niven was simply a bloody nice man brimming with social graces, who fell into the good life but didn't overlord anyone. Around midnight both agreed they could carry on with all this chat the following day.

Tom was taken to his room which was very small but had an en suite bathroom, and was near the stairs on the main floor. David's room was upstairs and perhaps twice as big as Tom's. They both hit the hay and fell into a dead sleep. David came into Tom's room at 0900 to wake him up. "Up, you lazy bugger," he yelled and hit Tom on the rump with a folded newspaper. "Let's have brekky on the verandah at 1000 shall we? Full English alright? (For those who may not know; full English is bacon, sausages, fried eggs, baked beans, perhaps a lamb and/or a pork chop, fried bread, grilled tomatoes and fried potatoes. Often followed with toast, marmalade and/or jam and quaffs of tea or maybe coffee). And all this is exactly what they had and finished by 1300, in time for a quick nap.

At 1700 David and Tom, extremely refreshed from their naps, sat down to discuss what the likely itinerary and daily routine might be, depending on whether gerry was cooperating or not. "I am not telling stories to the troops if gerry is shelling them at the same time," exclaimed David, " I would have to yell, and I have to nurse my voice, if you get my drift."

They pored over maps and diaries. David would now and then pick up the phone and ask for "12 unit," and discuss directions, or dates and times, then he would spring back to the table and scribble over the maps and make notes in a large log book. It was fun. And ice cold gin and tonics simply helped make it more fun.

This was August 1940 and another idyllic day passed. Tom realized that he had been so stressed for the past couple of weeks. It seemed just a few hours ago since they invaded Calais, when in fact, it was two months. He had been without sleep or much decent sleep anyway, and was now unwinding. His new boss was the reason he was feeling so much better, confident and ready to work. This war was very opposite to the war Tom had been in a few weeks or so before. He preferred this war.

The next day Tom was asked to bring the car around to the front. Along with a suitcase for himself for six days away. He had the servants place David's and his bags in the boot. At 0730 they were on their way. They were met at the gate by two armoured cars with four soldiers in each and an army vehicle, a Wolseley, with a driver and two "boffins" in the rear seat. This highly conspicuous convoy set off with Tom driving the shiny Humber and David in the front seat. They left the city to parts unknown. In fact they were headed in the direction of Phillipeville, close to the Tunisian border. "My God," exclaimed David, "this car is really such a pile of junk. What is it, a Humber? Hmmm! must be British. Aah well, one gets what one doesn't ask for, I suppose!"

Over 15,000 members of various allied troops had assembled just outside the town in a glow of sand and dust and smoke. The convoy with Tom in the middle car swerved off the main tarred road onto a dirt road that had been used by at least a thousand tanks. Armoured cars and soldiers' marching boots, so that it was quite smooth. About five miles on, they came across a large temporary arena with bleachers on three sides. It could perhaps seat seven thousand men. At one end was a stage, which was used all day long by various commanders to address various experts about various ideas. All ideas were on how best to kill Germans. Tonight, however, David Niven was going to address them with a bit of humour. There would be stories from home and abroad and he would then answer any questions the troops had. It was very obvious that these troops were part of the big push to get the Germans out of North Africa.

The Germans had been too successful so far and the allies needed a victory. The Americans were still being encouraged to join the war but had not done so yet. December 1941 and Pearl Harbour would change everything, but it was still long, long wait. The British really were mostly all alone. But there had been some leadership changes in North Africa and all the previous boffins had been killed, fired or quit. This was not India and this enemy was smart and powerful. new commanders needed to learn how to command in Africa. Optimism was in the air. Everyone knew a big and different push was on, no matter how dispersed the troops were. And with new allies joining every day, it was known to all the locals and eventually the Germans, that a very big battle was about to happen.

South African forces, who knew more about fighting in the climate and some tactics of the Germans, were quietly brought in to Eastern Algeria. With no ceremony and with their insignia hidden, they marched through the city of Constantine with hundreds of Arab kids begging for handouts: "Give me cigarette, South African," they yelled. Army HQ were infuriated that the South African's arrival was known. How did the Arab kids know they were South African? Military Police grabbed a couple of teenaged Arab boys and dragged them down to HQ and thoroughly interrogated them. "How did you know?" and "Who told you?" Well, the kids said they just looked at their feet and South African troops were the only allied forces who wore brown boots and everyone else wore black. "Didn't everyone know that" they asked.

Some men they thought were German, had asked them to come and tell them as soon as they saw troops wearing brown boots, as they were friends from South Africa. David Niven on hearing this, included parts of the story in his address to the troops. He said something like "Back home its loose lips that sink ships while over here it's brown boots that get you in the shit." The evening went well and Tom and David had a late dinner with some other men who had been in the "convoy". They dined on Roast Lamb with Apricots and Dates and drank a few bottles of Chateaunuf du Pape. By 2000 they were shown a tent for each one and by 2010 were both sound asleep.

They were both awakened at 0530 and had tea and biscuits brought to their tents with orders to pack and get the hell out of there by 0600. Both feeling somewhat groggy, Tom started the car and David jumped in to the front seat, with a Captain in the back seat reading out orders. Where to go, where to find fuel and where should they be by 1800 to repeat last night's performance, was all the Captain was trying to figure out. Later on, a British vehicle flagged them down and the Captain got out and into the other vehicle. "Well, you're on your own now. Constantine is a few hours south. There is an escort vehicle ahead although I doubt you'll need it as gerry is nowhere near us."

7

NOW THIS IS DIFFERENT

David asked Tom to "Find a decent bar along the way and stop as soon as you can. I want a Red Eye. I had one in Winnipeg in Canada once. Bloody great medicine for a hangover. Ice cold beer and a third is tomato juice. You should have one too. Try to find some Worcestershire Sauce 'cos it needs that extra kick."

"Yeah right!" replied Tom, "It sounds awful and you can have my share of the juice."

Around three in the afternoon they found a small village. There appeared to be about a dozen butcher shops. Each one had a dead camel carcass hanging outside it. The fanciest looking butcher, with a lime green front wall, also had a sign on the door with an arrow pointing to the back. The sign read "good meat food and with wine and cold beer".

"This is our oasis, Tom," begged David, "pull in here."

Tom swerved the big Humber to a halt and the two of them ran behind a big palm tree for a pee, and then behind the butcher and there they found a shady spot, with two or three goats, about six dogs and a buxom young lass about eighteen years of age, who just happened to be a barmaid.

"Get me four beers from the coldest part of your fridge and a bottle of tomato juice," said David in his veddy veddy put-on pompous-ass voice. "You wouldn't have any Woostah sauce would you?" (pronouncing the name the correct way, not using all four syllables).

"No jooose, no jooose," said the girl sadly "but camel head for lunch very good and cold beer."

"Oh well bugger the juice, and we'll skip lunch. Just hurry up with four beers and two glasses," retorted David mournfully. By now the escort vehicle had turned around and four soldiers joined the two and they too sat in the shade and drank cold beer and they too skipped the lunch.

The evening routine went on for three more nights. Arriving at barracks somewhere in Algeria. Tom parking the car and then slipping into the throng of troops to hear what David Niven had to say that night. It was always the same and yet tactfully different each night.

This night Niven regaled everyone with a story about Errol Flynn and making the film, 'The charge of the light brigade' (since told in David's book by the name "Bring on the empty horses" with the director, Michael Curtiz, back in the thirties).

Apparently him and Flynn would stand close to Curtiz and tease him about his lack of command of the

English language. One day he called out through his megaphone "Bring on the empty horses," when what he really wanted to say was for the riderless horses to be stampeded through the valley. When the duo pointed out his error, he fumed at both of them and yelled, "you think I know fuck nothing but let me tell you I know fuck all," at which point, exclaimed David, he and Flynn were rolling on the grass killing themselves laughing. About 8,000 troops that night were also rolling about and laughing. What a grand time. Warm air, young men, camaraderie and just plain fun.

The Luftwaffe, apparently living up to their reputation of having absolutely no sense of humour at all, decided to end this evening's fun by sending nine Stuka dive bombers over to bomb the makeshift arena. They had a siren on each plane and some stupid German pilot had his siren on way before the attack, thus alerting all and sundry, prematurely. Unfortunately for the Luftwaffe, the RAF had decided to have a night-flight exercise at 2000 and were seated in the cockpits of their Hurricanes when the scramble alert was given. Twelve Hurricanes were in the air just as the Stukas began their descent from 12,000 feet and began dropping their bombs.

The Stukas are a flawless machine for terrorizing their victims as they zoom down almost perfectly perpendicular until they reach about 500 feet. Once they release their bombs the pilots yank their stick back and pull up at a very sharp angle to quickly leave the scene of the crime. This exerts tremendous gravitational force on the pilot almost to the point of blackout. Regretfully one bomb fell directly on a group of allied soldiers who had assembled to maintain vehicles for a long drive in the morning. Eight British soldiers were killed and nearly a hundred were wounded. Twenty vehicles were also destroyed. Suddenly, the reality came back quickly to slap one in the face and to remind everyone that this was war. They had to go out and kill people if they didn't want to get killed themselves.

Fortunately, the Allies had access to open ports and bringing in replacement vehicles was just a matter of time. Replacing men was not as simple. Yes, it was math, but no, it wasn't just numbers. These were dead humans and they had to be collected, identified, wrapped up, and if possible shipped out back to England (unlikely) or buried right there, (more likely). Regardless, there was always a deep respect and ceremonial honour bestowed on every man lost.

Tom felt very strongly about how the men killed in action were treated. In this case of the eight men, the Commanding Officer wrote to each of the men's parents. Each letter was handwritten and came from the heart. In one he wrote "He was a fine young man and died being very brave, helping protect men from his unit. Due to his actions he saved many other lives. He will be buried here, without a coffin, as no wood is available in this part of the world. He will be wrapped in the flag of our regiment and will be saluted by the entire company at his funeral." Tom asked his Sergeant Major what sort of notice went out and he managed to get him a copy of what was said. Tom was impressed and frankly, thought every man should know how things happened and what was said after a battlefield fatality.

The British were pretty angry at being attacked which must have accounted for the accuracy of their anti-aircraft guns, as they shot down three Stukas. The Hurricanes, on the other hand, simply waited, hovering like Vultures, at about 4,000 feet until the remaining Stukas began their climb to safety. With their pilots still recovering from their blood pressure from the dive, they and their aircraft are at their most vulnerable.

Then the Hurricanes, a much sleeker and faster aircraft than a Stuka, swooped up in line, pointing upwards, and fired under the rear blind spot of each Stuka. The perfect dive bombers but useless dog fighters never stood a chance and not one made it. Every German plane crashed very close to where they had just been bombing and each was utterly destroyed. The result was considered a victory yet nobody was very gleeful at the outcome. The three German pilots who parachuted to safety, were captured immediately. One stupid arse, who must have believed all the Nazi propaganda back home about how the Luftwaffe were all supermen, pulled a Luger pistol from a shoulder holster. He started firing at the two British privates with bayoneted Enfield rifles who were approaching him cautiously. He obviously did not notice the British Major on his flank with a Sterling machine gun aimed at him. One burst from the Major and then there were only two live pilots. Both were quick-marched in front of the Major who was aiming his empty Sterling at them.

This means that he riddled the pilot with a full magazine of 28 bullets. Both surviving pilots were pushed inside a tent where several Intelligence officers questioned them. David went into that tent and stayed there for over three hours. Knowing he would not likely be driving anyone anywhere that night, Tom went to his tent and fell fast asleep.

8

A LITTLE R & R

David and Tom were together almost all day, every day, for another seven weeks, following the same routine. The allies had many camps set up as they waited for the call to attack, Meanwhile, there was practice and small arms training with marching and at night, a bit of entertainment from David Niven who always made them laugh.

One evening the soldiers put on a pantomime with almost as many in the cast as there was in the audience. One of the sketches was the "Swan Lake- Nutcracker Suite" as performed by the Radio City Hall Rockettes. David, probably the only person there who had ever been to New York, was asked to confirm the costumes were authentically American and everything else was in order. Of course, this examination was done on stage, in front of the audience and was milked for all it was worth. The "rockettes" wore long johns to enhance the beauty of their legs. David, slowly but surely examined each man, up the thighs, around the bust-line and now and then a firm grab of a half grapefruit, under a padded bra. Tom thought "Where would they find not one but a dozen bras?" Tom was persuaded to carry a pace stick under his arm and stand behind David, yelling at him to go faster, further, squeeze naughtier and the audience roared with laughter and for an hour or so, everyone forgot the war.

One night another company of men put on a fancy dress dance, dressing up half of the men as women in case they wanted a dance. David dressed as a goat, with Tom in the lead, under a blanket, and David holding a bag of black olives under his crotch. They all paraded in a circle and every now and then David would squeeze out a dozen or so olives onto the floor behind him. What men will do to get a laugh. The entire place was howling with laughter and everyone agreed it was a bloody fine night. Had David been in charge of **all** the armed forces, Tom said, he would have had Rommel and Churchill having a beer together and plotting how to overthrow Hitler.

But all good things must end, it seems. The next day was to be the last of Tom and David being a team. David told him he had to return to London and asked Tom to drive him to the airport after getting some sleep. It was a quiet, long drive back to Algiers. They noticed even in the sixty days or so that they had driven the other way, that at least triple the number of troops were now spread everywhere. It was now nearly September 1940.

Vehicles, mostly tanks, were lined up each side of the road. Tom guessed a thousand tanks at least. All Tom could think about was that gerry had better watch out. The Germans had been too successful and now they were going to be spanked very hard. Thank God I'm not in it Tom reflected. The two friends exchanged addresses and then shook hands. A brief hug and then David boarded a Mitchell bomber after a sad goodbye to Tom.

Perhaps David knew something and possibly believed he would never see his old driver again. Tom watched as smoke belched out from both engines after running up the motors during pre-flight checking. This seemed to take forever with David scrunched at the small round window and Tom standing on the running board of the car, both waving. The Mitchell taxied to the runway, sped down it until take-off and then a slow climb out over the ocean, and a safe journey to England.

Tom felt very alone and dismal. He was now the driver of a very nice car and frankly expected to be told to report somewhere else and drive somebody else. He figured he should find out where to report to among the apparent chaos of the Allied forces, which now outnumbered the camels.

Even British signs were put up outside some tents and shacks: "Av a cuppa just like 'ome" read one, "Toast n Tea, just like 'ome" read another. Tom was in need of a good cuppa, so he parked outside a shack, hoping to have a chat with some of the boys in there. But what he found was typewriters and blokes running around listening to the radio. They were communications branches of various forces disguised as cafes. Why? Who knows? Tom was immediately thrown out. "Sorry corporal, get yer arse in gear and 'op it," roared a Sergeant at Tom, "go and see the Adjutant down the road. He'll be in the second floor lounge of the hotel Americano near the well. Look for it yerself".

Tom parked the car in the shade next to the Americano Hotel. It was a seedy three-storey faded tangerine-coloured building, with shifty characters in fez's, standing around the front doors. They were neither in the hotel nor out of the hotel, just around the front doors. Tom eased himself through the mob and up to the main office. "Is the adjutant here?" asked Tom, and then spotted the same red haired man who had met him at the airport some four weeks before.

"Aah yes it's you Gale. Glad you're back. We need the car so make sure it's clean, filled with petrol but otherwise empty, then report back to me by 1600. Alright old chap?"

It was just noon so Tom ran down stairs and managed to get the car to a local military transport depot who allowed him to fill up and wash down the Humber. He unpacked his kitbag and took it back into the hotel, where he asked the manager to store it for him for about three hours. Then he rushed off to find any place that would feed him and get him a decent cup of tea.

He found about a dozen Brits under the shade of a clump of palm trees about two blocks from the hotel, where some enterprising local had opened a "famoos englis café." The sign may well have been written in camel dung and it was on the side of an old advert for sunlight soap, but the tea was real and the fried egg sandwiches were greasy but oh so tasty and the company of other soldiers was welcomed. Tom found himself unwinding and had a feeling of contentment with these men.

9

BACK TO THE WAR

About 1600 Tom excused himself. "Sorry mates, I regret I cannot stay with you to be your soloist in your song "Any Old Iron," in spite of my golden syrup voice. I know it's a disappointment for you all, but I am outta here. Goodbye. You'll get over it." He made his way back to the Adjutant's office. He sat down on a rickety chair just outside the office, where the officers were behind mile high piles of files. Payroll perhaps or maybe service manuals for tanks and lorries? Lots of paper anyway. Oh no, thought Tom, I bet they'll shove me behind a bleedin desk, make me a chief clerk perhaps, What a bloody come-down. I bet they take away my Humber and let some other bloke drive it. I'll be a little nancy boy getting tea for the brass and filing crap for a living.

Almost on the dot of 1600 the Adjutant popped his head out of the office door, nodded at Tom and said "Come in, old chap. Can I get you a cup of tea?".

Tom replied "No, but I think I need a toilet . Mind if I rush off there and then we can discuss my career advancement?" He got permission and was back shortly thereafter.

Then Adjutant Barry Heathshaw said, "I have news that you're not going to like, they want you fighting. They need battle hardened, trained and well rested troops. There aren't many like you, Tom, and you have all the qualities they need. Sorry, my man, but I have arranged some new kit for you, however, you will now carry the rank of Sergeant. By the way that is an extra two shillings pay a month so don't spend it all at once."

Tom chuckled a bit and asked, "Do you Adjutants all go to the same training school, because that is exactly what the last Adjutant said to me as he gave me a pay raise."

"Yeees" replied Heathshaw "we do".

"And what is it I am going to be a doing of?" asked Tom

"Well we understand you know about driving and flying. Tomorrow night we are loading thirty aircraft with troops to get in a bit closer to where we intend to make a stand. I'm afraid we have taken away your car and given you a rifle. Don't worry too much, the plane will be landing so you won't have to parachute out of it. Now then, any questions? I'll have someone run you over to your new group and you'll get there in time for a quick briefing and maybe a quick visit to the Sergeants mess for any decent left-overs from dinner. Goodbye Gale, nice to have known you, and here is your battle dress jacket with your new stripes already sewn on. Good luck, old boy."

Tom was summoned by a Colonel who was being driven off somewhere and he called out to Tom, "Are you Sergeant Gale?" Tom almost looked behind him forgetting that indeed he was now a Sergeant. "I agreed to share my car with you as you are not only going to our camp, but when you get there you need to see me anyway so I can fill you in on a special project. We can do most of that in my car. Sometimes things go right. Here we are, jump in. I am Colonel Dowdall by the way, pleased to meet you Gale." Tom threw his kitbag, along with the Colonel's kit, into the boot of the grey Vanguard saloon and the driver jerked forward and sped away. Basically, Tom was nothing special at all but many of the troops had never been under fire, so Tom was being given some goals HQ wanted achieved prior to a big push against Rommel, intended for who knows when.

"Mostly, Tom, you would be squad leader of twenty-one men in half-track armoured vehicles practicing the "Pincer Movement against the Germans," explained Colonel Dowdall. "You will have a piss-pot full of armaments and three men in seven vehicles. A 30 MM mounted anti-tank gun will be mounted on top. Each man will be armed with a Sterling machine gun and twenty clips of twenty- eight rounds each.

When you suspect gerry is in the area you will find his position, or you will be told his position by recon RAF, who may have spotted them from the air. In any event, once you know by any method available where they are, how many there are, what direction they are headed in and what speed they are moving at, I will inform each Pincer group. Then I can say which attack method to use, and from which direction. We haven't been as smart as gerry in the battles to date. We thought he would crumble and we never thought Intel was as important as we now know it is. Frankly, Rommel was smarter than we were and better armed, but times change. The old bugger is going to be given a hard lesson and he will not be able to escape."

Tom liked this man, Dowdall, and appreciated that he, unlike some leaders before him, was a well-trained, battle-hardened officer who had learned from his previous commander's mistakes, and having learned how to correct them, he would now overcome them. So far, Tom could not think of any questions. Colonel Dowdall certainly sounded like he had a plan and that plan was going to work.

Dowdall continued, "We know that Rommel is cunning but he also is a firm believer in 'if it works don't fix it.' He has beaten the hell out of us since this war began and his tactics were the reason. We can only pray that he does not decide to change those tactics, because our battle plan relies on him sticking to his tried and true methods. We have had remarkable success in our Intelligence gathering, and the Italians helped a lot. Frankly I don't think their heart is in it. I believe they would rather be in a British POW camp than out here fighting for their country and especially, fighting for Germany. Anyway, our plans are sound, Gale, and you should be proud to be on the winning side even though there will be some setbacks. We will prevail and the war will end soon".

It was almost two hours of driving when the view ahead became congested with vehicles and men and tents and shacks. "Well, here we are, Gale. I have papers for you to sign and some last minute details, so come into my quarters and someone will fetch you and show you to yours, in about an hour."

Tom grabbed his bag from the car and entered a pre-fabricated shack which had two rooms and a toilet. One room was obviously the bedroom, some six feet wide by eight feet long. The other room was an office with a desk and three rickety dining room chairs, a small toilet and sink in a room hardly big enough to hold them was across from the bedroom. Tom was told to sit and wait.

Soon Colonel Dowdall summoned him and said, "Keep this to yourself, Gale, I do not, I repeat not want to have this get around, you understand? Just tell me, what was David Niven really like? You see, part of our Intel Ops. came from him and they really have helped us learn a lot about the enemy. Did he ever reveal anything about his methods?"

Tom looked around the room and leaned forward. In a hushed voice he explained, "Actually, David told me everything. Each night he would show me his notes and how he would do such and such, if he were in charge. Then over lots of gin and tonics if it was at night and scalding hot tea if we were huddled over the secret papers during the day, we discussed how I would act and compared foot-soldier's methods versus those of an officer!"

Dowdall lost a few pints of blood from his face, as his mouth opened wider. "What sort of secrets did you discuss?" he blurted.

"Oh I swore, after I swallowed all the bits of paper, that if I ever told anyone, I would have to kill them," grinned Tom. Dowdall realized he had been duped and finally chortled. He had bought the entire story up 'til then.

Grinning from ear to ear Dowdall said, "Alright then, Tom, no more wanking around. Here's what you are to do. We have many weeks of planning ahead of us. Get yourself over to the Sergeants' quarters and use any reason you can invent to go and mix with the men. Some of them are, I believe, from some of your old outfits. Say you want to find them to catch up with old home gossip. But in any event, check out these men carefully. You are in charge of a unit of men who need to be fighters, brave, loyal and perhaps with more initiative than the average bloke. They must know nothing but in three days you are to give me a list of the twenty-one men you want on your team. If you don't find a decent Corporal then you name one man and I will promote him. I can't tell you how strong this team has to be. You are my Team Number Two, like a wing man in the RAF. You are to guard my flank 'cos I am in Number One position. Various numbers will be behind and around us, never less than five teams and up to ten."

Then, using a small tablecloth lying on a small table, likely his dinner table thought Tom, Dowdall wiped a blackboard clean and started drawing battle plans. "Look, we are here," and drew a crab-like picture. "We are the main body and we will be in American made half-track armoured and very fast vehicles. Gerry relies heavily on tanks. And tank for tank they kill us too easily with their

88 MM gun. Our tanks have half that sized gun, but we are much more maneuverable. We get around them, let's say there are eight of them, we surround them and split them up. We can knock them out with our 39 MM gun if we aim for the gap under their turtle like tops, or their tracks. If they stop and the crew spill out shooting, we take them out with Bren guns, or Sterlings, at close range. Then our light tanks can come in and finish off any just slightly damaged. The trick is not to allow gerry to confront us face on because one shot and we are gonners. How do you like it so far, Gale?"

"Well, I am glad you think I am important but I haven't the foggiest about this mission. You have explained it well and I believe I can pick out twenty-one good men. But this is a little different from jumping off a ship and trying to get across a beach, Sir. However, I get the point and let's hope gerry only sends in two tanks at first, so we can practice!"

Dowdall responded with, "Look old man it's a bloody war and we must do what we have to. This Rommel has some mystique about him but me thinks his luck is running out. We have new commanders coming and going; mostly going. Churchill is still looking for a great commander. He will find someone soon and give him anything he wants. The new American vehicles for example, are perfect for desert warfare and we get them and the Americans aren't even here yet. I say yet 'cos they will be soon."

Then they were interrupted by a Corporal, with a twangy Australian accent. "I'm here for Sergeant Gale to drive him over to his quarters in the Sergeants' mess. Can I have your kitbag Sergeant?"

Tom got into the front seat of a Jeep and in two minutes he was dropped off at the mess. He was shown his area, which he discovered he was sharing with another sergeant, a large man with a strange accent, from South Africa. Tom threw down his bag and greeted the man who was already lying on one of the two cots, "I presume the empty bed is mine, and by the way my name is Tom Gale," sticking out his hand".

The South African jumped up and pumped Tom's hand furiously "ja and my name is Pieter Joubert. Are you the bloke what's involved in some secret stuff?" Tom was shocked. Why would this be known? Not that it was such a great secret.

"Who said that?" asked Tom.

Pieter replied, "Aaghh! Never mind boet, your secret's safe with me and only some bloke out there said you knew all about brown boots and how they knew we were here from SA."

Tom said , "Listen, please keep this to yourself but we need to talk some more. I am just heading out to visit with some old chums from my home town in England. I'll be back later and let's get to know each other, okay?"

He found a group of rowdy soldiers, well, they all were rowdy but this lot were trying to get up some palm trees with bare feet, and betting a beer on each man who got the highest up the tree, more than fifteen feet and you got a beer. The purpose of this exercise was not known but as most men fell off at about the 10 foot high mark, the laughter made it appear extremely important.

Twenty yards away another group of about twenty men were racing lizards they had bought from Arab kids for a penny each. The rationale was that they gave the kids some money, they got to race a lizard, they could let it escape to freedom after the races were over and they made money on bets. What a perfect world. And how a little alcohol contributed to men's intelligence and fun.

Tom simply stood around and watched each group. He felt he shouldn't participate in these hi jinks anymore as he was now a Sergeant. In the good old days he would have had his lizard ready and his wallet out and been as rowdy as the rest of them. Now he started watching. Styles, personalities, tempers, cunning, guts in taking on that tree, and so on. He picked up enough mental information so that when he had a chance to speak to them, he knew a little about them from observation and could ask questions and determine which man might be who he would want on his team.

This was not Einstein's theory but it did show how Colonel Dowdall had thought out his game. Obviously, the army got the manpower that was conscripted. Training certainly helped to sort out promising individuals and fine tune a good soldier, but no matter what, in the end you fought alongside whomever was given to you if you were a team leader. The team concept gave a leader at least an opportunity to pick some bright sparks out of the group; ones you believed you could work with. And Tom already had selected over fifteen men he would put on his list.

For another day or so, Tom sat around and chatted with some men from his home town. He was very interested to hear that one of these men was a friend of Sergeant Pieter Joubert, Tom's new roommate. He was a language teacher and had been living in Bloemfontein, South Africa. He was fluent in Dutch and German and happened to be a dirt track motorcycle racer. He had once raced a BSA 500 in South Africa and won enough races from 1935 to 1940 that he made more of a living out of that than his government job teaching language. This Englishman, Larry "Dusty" White, had met Joubert at some function, in Bechuanaland, back in 1936. There Joubert was trying to gather money to protect the White Rhinoceros. Apparently, Chinese people thought the ground horn of the white rhino helped them with their erectile sexual problems and they were willing to pay big money for each horn. The indigenous natives were always seeking a way to make easy money, and poaching rhino was very lucrative.

Joubert and his cronies wanted to drug the rhinos and remove their horns, painlessly. Later on he told Tom that this was like a big fingernail so cutting did not hurt the animal. The drugging was so they laid still as you removed the horn. Joubert was also part of the anti-poaching unit and knew how to track, shoot and kill poachers. He had spent many hours hanging out of a half-ton truck, lassoing and then firing a dart into rhinos. Tom took notes. By now it was nearly 2100 and men were yawning and disappearing into tents. Tom went back to his quarters, with a list of twenty men he wanted. He had an idea who he would like as number twenty-one.

The Colonel was still awake and poring over maps and notes when Tom reported two days later. "C'mon in,

Tom, have a look here what we just discovered. Gerry is building up while he can. We have almost cut of his supplies entirely as the German Navy has not been able to get any sizeable fleet into the western Med. And we have Gibraltar guarding that entrance so east of Crete is about it for their supplies. We have good Intel that they want to make some sort of pre-emptive strike against us. We are going to make one against them and mess up all their grandiose plans. Now then, what have you been able to drum up out there regarding your team? I have five other Sergeants doing or having done the same thing. One day we shall all gather together and share ideas as well as get to know each other."

Tom said, "Well, as a matter of fact, I have twenty names on this list, but I have an idea which needs your approval. See, you think my number two man should be a Corporal. Well, it's like this, if you agree, I found a perfect bloke, but he is already a Sergeant, a South African one at that. I made some discreet enquiries and I know he has nothing to do with your plans. I have heard he is in charge of a motor unit maintenance group. He keeps their vehicles rolling. I believe that may be a very important job, but it would be a waste of talent to let him do that, and there are many more mechanics around. Now I have not spoken to him about this, and I suppose you could just order him to join up. But I would like to talk to him, feel him out and all that, knowing you would agree, if I get what I want".

Dowdall, shrugging some cigar ashes off his tunic said, "Well alright, I must say it's all bloody mysterious, Gale, but go and talk to him and let me know in the morning. This action will start in November, ish, some six weeks from now, so enough time to be ready. Okay, goodnight Tom".

Tom went back to his room and Sergeant Joubert was lying on the other cot now, reading a novel about dubious occupations of some women, somewhere. "Hey man, look, I am bigger than you and that cot is more comfortable but not as strong as this one, so if you don't mind I thought that one was better for you. Listen, we can exchange if you want."

Tom was pretty much exhausted and thought the man was right. "Pieter, thanks, the cot arrangement is fine, old chap. Tell me, are you off at early dawn somewhere tomorrow?"

"No man, I have this easy bloody job at the motor pool and I can go in any time before lunch. But they can call me anytime. Why so curious?"

"I have something to ask you and I am dog tired," pleaded Tom. "Can you and me chat over breakfast tomorrow morning?"

"Agreed," replied the rather affable South African. "First one awake wakes up the other, okay?"

They both were asleep within seconds, and fortunately their snoring was synchronized so they didn't annoy each other.

At least seven hours went by when the bugle call woke everyone up. Typical of a lot of men together, especially young fit men with energy to spare and little to do in between fighting and killing. They performed ablutions: yelling, swearing and competing with letting off gas. This daily routine was believed to be a plot by the armed forces, designed by the armed forces, to get men out of bed and onto the parade square or wherever else you were meant to be, at a very quick pace.

Sergeants Tom and Pieter smiled as they listened to the noise from the tent next door and made their way out to the Sergeants' mess and its relative tranquility. Apparently, soldiers stop farting when they get to be sergeants. With a plate of sausage and scrambled eggs along with a piece of charred toast and steaming hot and milky cups of tea, with four sugars each, they sat at the smallest table in the far corner.

"I don't want to beat around the bush, Pieter," said Tom. "I am a small part of a very interesting and thrilling operation. I am one of five or six sergeants with teams of them plus twenty-one men. Each other sergeant will be responsible for the same numbers in their team. The boffin who dreamed up this idea asked me to hand-select my team, and I am almost complete. I am also to choose a number two man, my wing-man if you like, to help me train and be part of a unit specifically designed to find a weak spot in enemy lines and attack and destroy them."

Pieter paid very close attention and shoved sausage down his face and rinsed it back with tea, as he concentrated on Tom's message, "Shit, that sounds bloody exciting" he said.

"Okay, so the original thought was to find a decent corporal to be my wing-man, but I heard about some of your exploits with rhinos and your skill at vehicle maintenance and I wondered if you might consider the job? And no, you would not be demoted to corporal. You stay the same but make no mistake, you would be having more fun and you would be in a crack unit. However, even though our ranks are the same, you would report to me. So whatcha think?"

"Tom, if I say yes will you tell me more details?" asked Pieter, "and could I change my mind if I didn't like the sound of those details?"

"Yes I will tell you every detail and no, once you've heard them, you cannot back out. Do you want to take a while to think about it, say an hour, 'cos I have to report in two hours to the bloke what's in charge of all this."

"Oh hell, I'll say yes right bloody now. Is it that Dowdall guy?" Pieter extended his hand, stood up and said "When my folks at home find out I'm working with a bloody Pommie, they will all throw up. But I am very pleased to work with you, Tom, and call me Piet".

At last Tom was over the gloom and feelings of loneliness after his separation from David Niven. He had a project he could get his teeth into, a boss who he got on with and twenty-one men who he felt would be a perfect close-knit bunch. He could contribute something and still enjoy the cameraderie of his "gang". Also Piet Joubert seemed like a perfect confidant who he would enjoy hanging around with.

With that, Tom ran over to Colonel Dowdall's quarters and told him everything. Dowdall beamed and welcomed Tom to his outfit. "We're now calling the project Operation Ragtag because of the personalities of most of you. Like you and Joubert, you're all a bunch of just the right kind of sods to get the job done. We want to experiment with part of the plan, this afternoon. Three teams of four cars each will head out south. One team will play hide and seek from the other two.

You will have five hours to go out and see if A and B can surprise and capture C. Tom, I want you to be A. Let's make this Joubert chappie in charge of B. Someone else will be C. He leaves an hour before you, at 1600. Be ready to move at 1700. Any questions, Gale?"

"I assume we are under strict battle conditions and not play-time, Sir, is that right?" asked Tom.

"Well of course, just no killing of our pretend enemy, members of unit C, OK, then get the vehicles and round up the men. I have already ordered twelve vehicles. We changed it from our original thought of three men in seven vehicles, as four, in each of four, per team, seemed more efficient. They are all readied and fully armed, and you need to now tell the men you chose what they are about to embark on, and they have, let's see, five hours to get ready. After this exercise we will gather all the other units, tomorrow, and discuss strategy and run some more tests."

10

NEW JOB AND NEW MATES

There was a flurry of activity as Piet and Tom scurried around and found the men selected for the task. Then Piet went down to the motor depot to make sure all the eight vehicles their two units would be using, were serviced, fueled, had spare petrol tanks on board, drinking water and so on. Unit C had already taken their four vehicles and left for parts unknown. All men in A and B Units were told to report at the depot at 1600, with no kit, except battle dress: Helmets, gloves and goggles, with sunglasses. And no more drinking alcohol as of then, well at least until the exercise was over.

The sun was so intense that every man took great care to avoid touching the metal on any part of the vehicles. Fortunately it was getting late and soon the sun would disappear over the horizon and then the heat would plummet and sweaters, gloves and headgear would be welcomed. The desert gets bloody cold after sunset. It only takes a few hours and you begin to shiver. Weather is a big part of war and the desert posed a very awkward climate.

It took a few minutes for the men to decide how they would divide themselves up into the four vehicles. Piet had not had the opportunity to hand-pick his team but they all seemed decent chaps with a sense of humour. Colonel Dowdall had picked the men and assigned them to Joubert in Unit B. They checked each other out and said things like, "I would rather be in the car ahead of Frosty 'cos; he farts all the time," piped up one soldier. Piet Joubert said, "Well in that case we shall have him in my vehicle up front and he can use his secret gas weapon on gerry. You will be in the very back vehicle, alright, err, what's your name?" A very handsome young, slender soldier replied, "Crosby, Sergeant, they call me Cherry and that position is perfect".

With a few small re-arranging tiffs as to who sat where, the men finally sorted out their preferences and which place on the vehicle was best to kill Germans. Tom's Unit A was ready, four cars with four men in each: Tom in A1, the rest in A2, A3 and so on. With lots of "yippee ay o" and "ride 'em cowboy" the two groups headed out of the camp in a cloud of dust, out to find Unit C, which was at least ten miles from them and likely in the valley just west of them. A and B would be riding into the sun while C waited for them and could see every move. Very smart defense by C. C had purposely let it be known they were headed for the valley and in a westerly direction, but actually they had headed for the gentle hills surrounding the valley more to the south. They would be a good thousand feet above the valley floor and could plan their retreat or attack with more knowledge of the "enemy".

They drove through the darkness, and in the desert that means pitch black. They had removed the connection from the tail lights and the headlights were taped over with black electrical tape with just a slit to allow light, if and when the headlights were ever turned on.

The sand choked them and stung their eyes as they struggled to keep on goggles and their scarves around their faces. They had about eight miles to go to the assumed "killing field", when they saw a brief light a few thousand yards ahead of them. Those stupid sods, thought Tom, someone in C just lit a cigarette or briefly turned on a light. He got on the radio to B and told them they had seen a light and was in pursuit to their right.

Finding anyone in the desert was difficult. At night almost impossible. It would not be like "keep on the A24 and take exit 237 to allawaquaddi," or some such place. There are no roads or pathways in the desert. If a tank patrol had driven there yesterday, the wind and sand would already have covered their tracks. So navigation is very important and the stars play an awfully useful means of knowing where you are and where you are headed.

Four hours went by and they had uncovered nothing. It was now about 2000 and they radioed that they had to stop for a pee break. Joubert and his B Unit slid to a stop behind Tom's unit and all the men jumped out and had a quick whiz as they shivered and chatted in hushed tones. Joubert was a little concerned. He sidled up to Tom and said, "There's something not quite right here, it's too damn quiet and, other than that brief light we saw back there, there's nothing. We lost the light, whatever it was, and we see and hear zip. We should have been on to them by now".

Tom agreed, but he had no real experience of this desert warfare, and besides, this exercise was part of his training. He replied to Joubert, "Look Piet, let's just do what we were supposed to do and if we don't find C, then we go home before dawn with our tails between our legs and get told off and we can do another exercise another day. Okay?"

Then in the far distance they heard the clanking sound of tracks. Heavy tracks like those on big tanks. Tanks that were not supposed to be in that area, and certainly not German tanks. Buttons were done up and men jumped into their respective vehicles. "What do you think Tom?" asked Piet, "split up and head for the noise as carefully as we can, me left and you right?"

Tom suggested, "Let's all go in single file. I'll lead and you follow very slowly so no corkscrew sand-dust flys up. Keep it under 10 mph. Once we see what it is and who they are and what direction they are headed, we can split up and flank them. Look here, if it is gerry and more than a dozen of them, let's just retreat as we will be slaughtered by those numbers. Less than a dozen, we attack, agreed?" Suddenly this playful little exercise had become a real situation, and where was C?

They drove slowly toward the last place they thought the clanking sound came from, and they came across a camel-back hill. They wedged their little convoy in between the two small humps and could see beyond to a vast, flat valley floor, about five miles long to the horizon and half a mile wide. The whole goddam valley was filled with German tanks, maybe 400 of them. They could be seen in the moonlight and were well camouflaged with no lights, except here and there, the glow of a cigar or cigarette.

Out of seemingly nowhere, Colonel Dowdall, who was C leader without anyone knowing, silently appeared, with his three half-tracks, behind them. Tom remembers that his sudden arrival, unannounced, "scared us shit-less". Dowdall jumped off his lead vehicle, which he was driving, and he, Piet and Tom huddled together a few yards from the rest of the men.

"I have been up on the crest of that hill back there, watching you blokes meandering around looking for me, when I caught sight of gerry and his tanks, driving into the valley, obviously looking for trouble".

Tom said, "Let's get the hell out of here while we can and we can warn the camp commander to prepare for an attack. We could be ready and waiting if we had about two hours notice. I vote we move back right now."

Piet agreed as did Dowdall. With that they all got into their vehicles and turned them around with Dowdall in the lead yelling, "Follow me in a straight line".

There was a pale mauve glow in the sky and dawn was approaching. That meant the Germans, if they were paying attention, would see them as a silhouette against the sky. It also meant they could run faster and get out of sight quickly and drive three times faster than any tank, and they did. Holding on for dear life and freezing in the cold air, they got up to 60 mph at times and soon were way ahead of the German tanks and getting very close to the main allied camp.

At 0500 they skidded into the main camp guard house and advised the night shift to raise the alarm for an impending attack, while Dowdall was on the phone to the commanding officer trying to get him woken up. "Who is this?" he yelled down the phone, "this is Colonel Dowdall and I want General Hargreaves woken this minute. How dare you, I have not been drinking and this is not a practical joke. When this is over I will be having your arse bent over my stove and whipping it with wet palm fronds. Now wake him up now do you understand?.... Oh! good morning, General Hargreaves, Sir. I am afraid gerry is on his way with at least 400 tanks. Maybe two hours. Yes, I know we have no tanks, but next door we have nearly 250 and we can surprise gerry if we move now. Yes Sir, I will contact them now and explain."

Hargreaves swung into action. His aide was on the phone and the radio, waking all and sundry up and getting them to battle stations. Actually, it had been Brigadier General Mitchell, arriving as the recently appointed new leader for North Africa. He had managed to park outside a General's quarters without anyone challenging him. He immediately instigated a battle station routine. He said, "We can always be attacked without much notice. We need to know where we should be and what we should be doing and cooperating in unison with every other soldier so we can defend ourselves and repel the huns without having to read a manual. Get practicing now".

By the time Dowdall had roused all five commanders, in both camps, the first of almost 30,000 men had fallen in and tanks were being started and manoeuvred into defensive positions. Sand bags, firearms, helmets and ammunition, were all checked and in the right place.

In an hour the entire two companies were at their stations and ready. The kitchen staff had already begun pouring out porridge and coffee for the men; sending three-man units out to each battle station so the men could fight with some nutrients inside them. It was a smooth, efficient, well-planned operation. All of it.

Regretfully it was all for naught. Quicker than anyone had thought, the Germans went around the two camps and simply drove in firing non-stop with their enormous 88 MM tank guns. The German half- tracks went in as soon as there were damages and wounded allies, and they finished the job. They destroyed everyone and everything. Maybe 100 British tanks were destroyed compared to 20 German tanks. Perhaps 800 allied troops were killed compared to some 200 Germans. It was a complete disaster for the allies. The Germans had the advantage of surprise, even though everyone knew they were coming. They arrived sooner than anticipated and from an unexpected direction. Their Panzer tanks were bigger and faster and with more accurate guns. They also had a huge single tank gun that was half again as big as the British tank gun, with three times the range. The Germans were made up from at least seven divisions of their North Afrika Corp. The allies had eight different regiments making up their forces in this battle.

Tom and Piet decided to get the hell out of there and drive to the largest allied camp, about ten miles away, where another 500 or so Sherman tanks, were stationed. The Germans had cut all telephone links and the radio, so there was no other way to inform the reserves. There was a gap in the perimeter and the Germans, amid the chaos of battle, did not see the two speed out through the dust and chaos toward the north. As soon as they were clear, about a mile away, they got onto their radio and flicked through every band, until they got a reply. The caller asked "Do you read me, over, we are company Delta, who are you?"

Piet replied, "Are you the blokes with the tanks? I am Sergeant Joubert of 25 battalion and we are in a huge battle."

"Yes we are Delta and we are a tank brigade. What do you need?"

"We need every bloody tank you have headed South to 25 Command as Gerry and his Panzers are there decimating our blokes. They have over 300 Panzers and they are at coordinates Map 4, Zulu 47 and Echo 29. Get ready and go now for Christ's sake, move," demanded Piet. All of this activity came about in minutes.

For a while it was just a drive in the cooling desert with a bunch of mates and all paid for by the army. Then, in an instant, the war was on and their lives were at stake, as well as those of thousands of their friends. Piet was spitting into the microphone. "Roger, understood, you are heading to Map 4, Zulu 47 and Echo 29." And that was the final message.

A long time ago, the British realized the Germans knew their every move, and must have been listening in to their radio transmissions. So, as those radio transmissions were vital, they developed a map code rather than use the latitude/longitude positioning, and thus the alpha/numeric system at least gave them some degree of secrecy. Now and then the allies also used a code they knew the Italians had stolen, so would hear and understand everything being planned, except it was all a pack of lies. And the Italians fell for it almost every time.

Tom waited as they pulled over to the side of the road. Time dragged on and the men huddled around their half-tracks and suddenly Tom told this funny story which entertained the men and kept everyone alert as they were in a precarious position. "Apparently," he started, "one time, earlier on in the war, the British army had only about twelve anti-aircraft guns all lined up along a four-mile stretch of road. All covered in camouflage netting. The problem was that number was nowhere near enough anti-aircraft guns for adequate protection. They should have had over a hundred. After a few beers and a lot of suggestions, the boys back then got a whole lot of telephone poles that they had retrieved from a ship. So they propped them up every few hundred yards and covered them with camouflage nets. Then they made sure the real guns were protruding out of their nets while the telephone poles were not.

Afterwards the HQ asked each zone for a sitrep (a situation report, by radio transmission, letting central command know about everything, such as injured men, fuel supplies, vehicles out of order, ammunition, food requirements, and so on). The radio buzzed and HQ asked "Zone A, your sitrep, and make sure we are not on a frequency that eyetie uses. All we need is a photo plane of theirs flying over to confirm our situation."

"A zone here. Exactly what situation are you talking about?"

"HQ here. Obviously you did not receive the warning yesterday. All our anti-aircraft guns are out of commission between 1300 and 1400 hours today, which means if those eyeties wanted to they could fly over and take pictures."

"A Zone here. Oh I see, well we wouldn't want that now, would we."

"And sure enough," continues Tom, "a Savoia-Marchetti SM-79, one of them three engine jobs, came flying low, and took pictures of all those AA guns. I bet they looked over those pictures and reported to their boffins. "Look how careless the British are. Look how many guns show through their camouflage netting. It's a good job we knew they were being serviced which gave us an easy opportunity to fly over and photograph them. The British have many AA guns and we should never try flying over the British camp, unless we have good intel like we had today."

The men all had a giggle at that story as the four cars waited, pulled off to the side of the rough terrain they called a road. They were exhausted and actually nodded off for a while. A noise and a huge cloud of smoke and sand emanating from hundreds of allied tanks heading out of the north, towards their command, or what remained of it, jolted them awake, and they watched with pride as their mates came rumbling forward.

Frankly this battle was a bloody nuisance. Yes, the allies wanted to finally get the Germans out of North Africa but they would have preferred that the timing be later. The allies had been bloodied for a long time now and they had yet to win any sizeable battle. And they were not quite ready for this one. The allies had their own plan and that was to first build up their forces, then train them, train them again with very real exercises and only then, seek out Rommel and hit him hard. It was not supposed to be in a short notice, unprepared panic, such as this.

The Germans knew their ability to get fuel and supplies were becoming increasingly difficult. As the allies slowly began seizing control of many North African ports, for the Germans too, the timing was crucial. If they did not start pushing the allies back beyond Algeria, they would be forced to start retreating back and eventually leave Libya and go home.

Tom often thought of the future of this part of the world. Talking to Piet and a couple of other men, during this quiet spell, he said, "How will the Arab population in the after-war world, feel about us and the Germans wrecking what little there is here? First the Italians come in here and treat the populace as a collective piece of shit, then the Germans come in here to help the Italians, but really to look the place over. "Hmm! lots of oil here, maybe a colony for us Germans," I'm sure this would cross their minds. Then we come in here to stop the axis troops from running the place. The Arabs, well, excluding Egypt who don't believe they are Arabs, are really all caught up in this power struggle, with helplessness as they have no say in it at all.

I bet fifty years from now, there will be in-fighting among all the Arab countries. They will hate each other, probably because of differing religious points of view, but collectively we'll get the blame. They will blame the British, El Awrence and King Feisal and all that. They will destroy anything that is British. If the Germans win, there is no way the Arabs would even dare to go after them, as they would be quashed like the cockroaches the Nazis believe them to be. At best, there would be five or six countries claimed by the Italians and the Germans, and run as dictatorships, and the Arabs would be treated with no mercy. If we win, the Arabs will be wanting hand-outs from the allies, and then when they are happy with the money they get from us, they will take charge of the oil, and then gangs will go around and destroy anything that looks European. They will destroy everything they have and back into pre-Christianity savagery. I'll tell you what, my son," Tom continued to all listening, especially Piet, "I hope I don't die and get buried here, because one day they will piss on all the allies graves, or bulldoze them out of existence. Please let me be buried in England."

"Okay, yes, there is a problem," answered Piet. "Do we leave all the countries where there has been no progress at all, like South Africa. You know there was, by comparison to other countries in the world, absolutely no rule of law, no real religion and absolutely no buildings erected, and no written language, when the Dutch arrived in South Africa in 1652. There was only tribal-ism. No rules about owning or trading land, or any rules about any business, as there was none. If a man owned two cows and needed a basket of fish, he would never think of asking a fisherman for a trade. The men would fight and the winner had both cows and all the fish and the loser was dead. Now, already, there are stirrings from the natives that the white man has all the goods and they have nothing. So, like here, one day it is going to be simple. If you have all the goods then instead of showing me how I could get some too, why don't I just kill you and then all the goods are mine? I will own everything. I won't know what to do with it all but it will be mine. You just wait and see!"

"I see your point" replied Tom, "but here we are right now and we are caught up in a kill-or-be-killed war. Now what?"

The men knew they had to now join in and get to the killing field, but clearly they had to make a plan. They had a lot on their minds. Tom and Piet had some inter-esting philosophical arguments that nobody disagreed with but the subject matter wouldn't just go away. Each man would remember the comments, perhaps for the rest of their lives, and that wouldn't be much longer if they didn't get going.

11

UNCONTROLLED CHAOS

Tom and Piet, being the two leaders, now had a big dilemma on their hands. What the bloody hell should they do now? How could they contribute? They couldn't just sit on the side of the road. The tanks should be able to do the job without their help and they couldn't do much with their relatively puny weapons up against a Panzer tank. "Our goddam weapons are for personnel not tanks," exclaimed Piet. "How the hell can we use these effectively?"

"That's the answer" piped up the Lance Corporal in Tom's unit, "our bloody tanks are going to blast a couple of hundred of gerry's and their occupants are going to be scrambling out, as well as their infantry will be running around all over the place. We can circle them and move away from the tanks quicker than they can turn a turret. Then we kill the bastards as they run away from their burning vehicles."

"We can drive around a Panzer's turning turret, faster than they can turn it. They will know we are nearby but won't know where," another man suggested, "then we can get at their tracks and as long as another tank nearby doesn't have full view of us, we can stop them dead."

"Right, that's what we'll do, make a bloody nuisance of ourselves," Tom said, "we can do a lot of damage. We can find targets and lead some of our tanks to where gerry is hiding. Also we can protect any of our blokes who are scrambling out of their tanks, as well as shoot all those German sods running around. We should split up when we get closer and do what needs a doing of. Let's go and good luck, watch your backs. No stopping for a chat unless we run into Unit C somewhere and we can explain what it is we are attempting to do."

The eight half-tracks sped off and overtook the allied tanks before they reached the killing ground. The battle was slowing down with a clear German victory when the first of the now four hundred allied Sherman tanks came over the ridge. The axis knew they were now in trouble as they were almost depleted of fuel and ammunition. Mostly what they had was a large number of infantry, maybe eight or nine thousand, running over any allied troops and with their MG42's, killing any survivors from a destroyed tank. Plus they still had about 200 Panzers, which were almost powerless because of fuel and ammunition shortages. There was a lot of hand-to-hand battle. The Brits were angry; they had been receiving messages about what the Luftwaffe was doing to their families back in England. They wanted every bloody German dead and they didn't care how.

The number three vehicle in Tom's unit A drove up to four burning Panzers, and every man jumped out of their half-track and, using grenades, leaped up on a Panzer tank and pushed primed grenades through any vent and then waited for the main hatch to open. An explosion would occur, probably killing one or two occupants, then with screams and pleading the rest of the tank crew came tumbling out, hands raised, "kamerade, kamerade", they yelled.

But stories had been told that in previous occurrences these bloody German tank buggers had been captured and before they could be searched, they had pistols and shot some of their captors. This was not going to happen again. They were shot.

The idea was to take them prisoner but that never happened. One German took out a pistol and shot at one of Tom's men, Mickey O'Brien, and shot his wrist watch off his arm. Mickey's pal, right beside him, blasted the German to smithereens with half his clip on an old Sten gun he loved to carry. From then on nobody was given a chance. They were mostly put out of their misery, as they would likely die from burn wounds received when their tank was disabled earlier. Certainly there were no ambulances and medics around to treat the wounded. Well, there were but nowhere near enough.

Tank battles are not as squeaky clean as say, dropping bombs from 30,000 feet. Perhaps the victims might disagree? A pilot never sees, close up, the devastation caused by his strafing and bombing, and furthermore, gets to go back and have a cup of tea when it's done. This is not to discredit the danger and exhaustion of a pilot's work, however.

The battle continued for hours and then the "Texas Rangers" came to the rescue. Many of the Nazi infantry saw the allied tanks arriving over the dunes and started to retreat back to the east, from whence they had emerged hours ago. They had set out looking for mischief, trying to destroy the allies in small decisive battles, one small camp at a time. Not only had the Germans not realized that this first camp had so many tanks, but failed to realize how many the Brits had in another camp just ten miles away. They had only two choices: they could stand and fight, or flee. They chose the wrong one, they stood their ground. They could only see a column of Sherman tanks in a row eight wide, coming through the pass and not knowing there was about fifty such rows behind them. By then many of the German infantry had fled through the back exit of the valley where they believed they would have an easy escape home to their major base, some eighty miles east.

All would have gone well except as they ran through the gap between the two hills, there were ten British half-tracks armed to the teeth, waiting for them. There were too many Germans for the forty allies to take prisoner if the Germans had succumbed or surrendered, so a battle commenced.

Unit A's first half track simply charged straight for the line which scattered gerry everywhere. The other half-tracks drove outwards and then back into the column with every weapon blazing. It wasn't quite one sided but over five hundred German foot soldiers were killed that morning, with a loss of three half-track vehicles and fifteen men of Tom's unit.

Piet Joubert was slightly injured when his half-track rolled over after being hit by a German hand grenade, and four of his men in the vehicle were killed either by the grenade or the rollover. The scene was chaotic, A and B units were running out of fuel and ammunition and there was nowhere to go to replenish.

The German infantry was no longer a real target as many had run back to the relative safety of their beloved Panzers, even though the Sherman's were now pummeling the Panzers, because they had fuel and were far more maneuverable. Still, the Panzers were no easy pushover and the score was gerry down to about 140 Panzers and the Brits down to about 350 Sherman's.

The radio traffic between tank commanders was tense and fast. They were almost at a stalemate and the consensus was that if they gathered together and left a way for the Germans to retreat, they would. The Germans wouldn't believe their good fortune at the Allies move which enabled them to retreat to return another day to completely defeat the allies.

Meanwhile, the Allies were also running low on fuel and ammunition, as this battle had been so spontaneous, planning for supplies had not been a priority. And so, when the Germans saw their opportunity to run, they did so. They left behind over a thousand injured men and over two hundred completely destroyed tanks, mostly Panzers. Of course the Allies could have chased them but then all they would have accomplished was to create another killing ground and frankly, they wanted the big battle which was soon to come, to be on their terms.

This battle gave the Germans some food for thought. This was the very first time that they had not decimated the British and it scared them. When they compared losses, against fewer infantry and less tanks plus the advantage of surprise, they were shocked. Their final losses that day were over five hundred men killed and over a thousand injured who would now become Prisoners of war. Certainly, Rommel could see the pendulum swinging slowly but surely to another direction. The number one man in his absence had just died from a car accident, a week before. The timing was right and Rommel now wanted the Allies out back as far as Algeria, or more, out of Africa altogether. But first he wanted Tunisia. The Allies had a different agenda.

When Tom gathered together what was left of units A and B, he had Piet Joubert on his vehicle and his total group was now six half-tracks and fourteen men. He left two men with one half-track and told them to stay where they were with the injured and dead men and he would get medics to them very soon, perhaps two hours at the most. Piet's injury was from a shard of metal, likely from a grenade, that had sliced open his face and removed some upper teeth; not life threatening but messy and bloody painful.

Piet tried to talk and mumbled "Why couldn't I get shot in the arse, like my cousin on the Limpopo river?"

"For God's sake," yelled Tom, "can't you just shut up for once and enjoy the view?"

In fact they were travelling too far north and pretty soon realized they were lost. No navigational equipment, even a pocket compass. Maps had not been secured during battle and most were thrown out of the vehicles. So they judged by the sun which way to drive. Now it was about 1500 and they saw a column of dust ahead, and, assuming this was an Allied force, they drove straight at them.

Forty minutes late they realized they had stumbled on to a unit of patrolling Germans. Now this was exactly what their group had been organized to do. And, as there were no tanks the job would be much easier. "Piet you are going to have to hang on a bit my friend" yelled Tom, "we are going in for a fight".

"Don't bother about me," gurgled Piet, "just kill the bastards for me."

They went behind the column of trucks and split up, with three cars on one side coming at the Germans flank from the west and Tom's from the east. They roared in, perhaps caught up in their successes and the adrenalin pumping through them, they were not quite as cautious as they should have been. As they got to their target, they saw four more vehicles that were armoured and hidden in the huge dust clouds; and they realized then they would simply be committing suicide if they attacked the enemy. They had run into a German patrol who were looking for their tanks that should have been return-ing to base soon. There were seven large trucks, maybe three tons each and four men in each truck, plus, four SD.KFC light armoured vehicles. Simply too much to start a fight without the element of surprise. They were outnumbered four to one. But also against more and far superior vehicles.

It was too late to just turn around and flee, so surrender was the only choice. They halted their advance and waved a white shirt. One of the trucks came over to Tom and his party of brave but not foolish men. The other German vehicles slowly drifted over and surrounded the British. And so in just over a year, Tom was again a POW. "That's me," said Tom, "I can never get anything right the first time. This time I might become the professional POW that gerry obviously wants me to become!"

Christmas had come and gone with no parcels or even a decent dinner. It had occurred some weeks ago but the pace of this war was furious and there was little time for festivities. Here it was now, nearly Easter 1941 and he was back in the care of the Germans.

12

NOT AGAIN

The German officer in charge was an NCO, a Sergeant Major, who introduced himself as Gunter Heisman. He knew a little English and said, "you are now my Prisoners. If you respect my job I will respect your position in life and will treat you well. Any, how do you say, bullshit, and I vill shoot you without even a trial. Understand all of you raise your hands."

The two other NCO's also chatted with the leader and it became obvious that one truck would be sent back with the Sergeant and two men, while the patrol would carry on south west to discover what the Allies were up to and where their large tank battalion had disappeared to.

The Germans took all the half-tracks and all the weapons, closely examining, with great enthusiasm and surprised looks, each weapon and its functions. Using the enemy's vehicles was very common on both sides in

North Africa. This practice enabled many an attack to occur with surprise because of the visibility problems, caused by the sand. Just when the vehicles could be recognized, it was assumed they were friendly, until the very last moment. It was pretty certain that the Allied vehicles, now in the German's possession, would, one day be used in this manner.

Piet was attended to by a German medic who had morphine and some greasy stuff which he put in Piet's mouth. Then Piet got five stitches and was gently lifted into the truck and placed on a bed of sorts, made from burlap bags and cardboard sheets. Then the rest of the Brits were told to climb up into the truck and sit as close to the front as they could, on two benches that ran either side. These were obviously troop carriers and, as such, were fairly comfortable, "But not a bleedin' footrest in sight," moaned Tom.

The German truck, loaded with POW's, did a large swooping turn on the flat desert bed and headed back in the direction it came from. One Corporal was driving. The German Sergeant Major was up front seated next to the driver and one private was seated in the back, an M42 resting on his lap, aimed at the fourteen prisoners.

"Can we talk?" one of the men asked the German private, with a lot of charades which presumably meant talking. "Ya, Ya, the German said, "okay you can talk to each other."

"Jesus Christ, what a bloody day we've had. Well, two days, actually," moaned one private.

"Well yes, but remember the fate of a couple of hundred men back there who won't have another day, ever. Poor sods," piped up another man.

"Best guess as to where we are going?" asked another."Tom, you've been through this before, what will happen to us now?"

Tom, pretending to hold something like a football in his hands replied "Oh look my crystal ball is still intact. I can see it all now, behind bars in jail for the rest of the war. How the bloody hell do I know?"

By then it was 2200 and the desert was getting cold. The truck was moving fast, at least 50 mph, across the very smooth and flat desert. Once again, one man, a tall private from Dorchester, Chuck McGrall, said to Tom that he knew a little German.

"If they say anything of interest and I can figure out what it is I will pass it on." Tom explained how he was with a similar situation the last time this happened and the translation really helped.

Most of the men were somber. Tom seemed more worried about this capture. For some inexplicable reason, when he was first captured in France, the war had just begun and it didn't seem as serious. Even though his unit then was almost totally wiped out, and the carnage and brutality was everywhere, most of their post-capture seemed like a lark. This time, he felt a sense of foreboding he had never felt before. They drove for hours. The sky was beginning to take on that pale mauve, then a yellowish tinge the sun struggled to fight the cold and rise over the distant hills to give some warmth to the earth.

The men were shivering with their teeth rattling, not just because of the temperature but the wind created by the fast moving vehicle found every crack in the canvas and every place where the metal did not match up. Those little cracks and that innocent half-inch gap became a howling icy wind. Nobody was in any mood to crack jokes or, heaven forbid, sing. They wrapped themselves in paper or cardboard and stuck handkerchiefs down their collars in a futile attempt to stop their teeth from chattering. The apprehension did not make it better.

They periodically examined Piet Joubert, who was out cold. Fortunately for him the morphine had done its job and he stayed unconscious for most of the trip. They never stopped once. One soldier noticed a sack under Piet's feet and he thought he might find something in there to eat. He was right; it was their own small supply of food and the Germans had tossed it into the back of the truck.

Inside the sack was the most delectable assortment of British Army gourmet delights. There was four tins of Argentinean corned beef, one tin of Canadian sweet, thick condensed milk along with half a dozen tins of Norwegian pilchards, "in a rich tomato sauce". They were all astonished and immediately yelled at the lone, equally cold, German guard. "Is it okay if we eat this food? " Someone asked, "You want some too?"

The guard responded, "Eat okay, me no. English food shit!"

Tom was about to retort with "'ave you tried sauerkraut?" but decided to eat and shut up.

109

All the tins had metal tabs on them so easy to open, except the milk, but then, when would anyone eat that milk? So all tins were opened and, because their bayonets had been seized they used their fingers. Three fingers together into the tin and scoop out a "sclunge" of bully beef and slurp it down. It was awkward but after a bit of practice you could lift a whole pilchard out of the flat oval tin and drink down a bit of the tomato sauce. Sustenance was important here, not style. Condensed milk had two holes bashed into the top, using a metal rod found on the truck floor, The tin was passed round, as had the other two entrees, and everyone had a slurp; truly a dessert to remember. A more nauseating trio of food no one could imagine. Fortunately, it was just once and there was just enough to make everyone feel a bit stronger and not quite as cold.

Someone yelled out that it was 0630 and by then the sun was blinding the driver as it shone almost parallel to the desert floor, right into his eyes. The truck began slowing down to perhaps 25 mph, and Tom asked the guard if he could stand up and look out of the front canvas flap. It seemed no big deal to the guard so Tom managed to ease his creaking knees into a standing position. He commenced with a few exercises, bending legs, standing on toes, standing on one leg and wiggling the other, and so on, just to get the circulation started. Then he popped open the canvas flap and the incoming air was fresh. It was not quite as cold as during the night and he noticed the sun was off slightly to the right, so they had turned left and slightly to the north. Here there were more small shrubs and a very flat desert floor.

Tom could make out in the distance, a lot of vehicles, maybe 1,000 and a huge barbed wire area, with a dozen or more black Mercedes cars with swastikas flying at the front of each one. You didn't need to be a military scholar to know something big was going on and some very serious brass were attending a meeting about something. Possibly 20,000 troops, or more, were all seated eating breakfast.

Tom said, without addressing anyone in particular, "Where did the bloody enemy get the tables and chairs? If it were a British breakfast they would be sitting cross-legged on the sand eating out of a metal dish. Gerry has cutlery and plates, seated at tables as far as the eye could see. Did they have some bloody moving van just to hold the tables and chairs and the cutlery and crockery? How do they manage to be so organized compared to us?" As they drew closer, all the POW's were pushing in to see out the front and witness this enormous army poised for some tremendously important battle. All must have wondered if their own forces could repel such a huge and well-fitted army.

The truck pulled up near a barbed wire fence and the Sergeant Major, who was likely dozing comfortably in the front of the truck where it was nice and warm, suddenly became "leader of the world", Tom recalls. "He became a pompous ass, pointing and strutting about. "Alright Englanders, jump off the truck right now and form up here." He had his pace stick and waved it around like a drunken orchestra leader.

Then he yelled, "You, yes you, Corporal," at one hapless German soldier who looked like he was sneaking off back to his sleeping quarters. "Whatever you are doing, stop. Guard these British soldiers and open that gate. Then help my men get all of them into that area behind that fence and then lock the gate. Take out the wounded man and have him taken to the field hospital with one of the POW's who can explain to the hospital staff what has happened to him and what treatment he has received so far, understood?"

At that moment, a man stood up at the officer's table (they were the only soldiers wearing black or field grey, so unless they were planning a fight in a coal mine they were officers.) He was of medium height and a barrel-chested, extremely erect man, with medals down both sides of his chest and a very large Iron Cross swaying around his neck. His hair was thinning and he marched about 100 feet or so, up to the truck.

"Sergeant Major," he asked in a very authoritative tone, "wer sind diese manner and wus tun sie mit ihnen zu tun planen ?" (who are these men and what are your plans for them.) The entire conversation was in German, but Tom was getting the gist of it translated from his own interpreter.

The Sergeant Major paled a little and clicked his heels so hard his ankle bones nearly snapped. He was being addressed, one-on-one by somebody close to the Messiah. He blurted out, "Well, Sir, they are all British army soldiers, captured yesterday close to the Algerian border. I have placed them in the stockade and then I will feed my men, there are only three of us. I will then have the prisoners fed and after that have them inter-rogated and their place of detention determined."

"Yes, alright, but first you feed the prisoners and then you feed your men. Is that understood?" He said in a stern tone but not so as to belittle the Sergeant Major in front of his men, or in front of the POW's. Then he turned to the POW's and, wiping his mouth with a ser-viette, said in perfect English, "Gentlemen, I am Erwin Rommel, perhaps you have heard of me. I am sorry about this but this is war and this same scene could be happen-ing right now where my men have been captured, out there somewhere, by your men. You will be well treated by my men and according to the Geneva Convention. You must not worry. We can send information to your loved ones via Portugal and then you can rest up until this war is over and that will be not long to wait, I assure you. Now, please do what you are told and enjoy a hot meal. I am sorry, no 'full English breakfast" as you say, but nutritional. Look at how our food keeps my men winning every battle. Who knows what it could do for you?"

Then he saluted and said, "Goodbye, I hope we can meet again under better circumstances." He reached out to Tom, who had been in the front of the group. Tom saluted and Rommel shook his hand quite vigorously and then marched off back to his fellow officers, still seated at the large officer's table. Tom couldn't believe it. Firstly, where the hell did all these officers come from? There must have been thirty or more and none seemed to be below the rank of General. Secondly, to have personally met Rommel was a real note in Tom's mental diary.

Years later Tom recalled, "That Rommel was a much nicer bloke than Monty, (referring to Field

Marshall Montgomery, still to arrive on the scene, Rommel's nemesis).

Piet Joubert was still unconscious, when he was taken away on a stretcher, carried by four German soldiers wearing white hospital coats and accompanied by a young Yorkshireman, Teddy Broomhouse, who was to be the designated explainer to the German medical officials as to what happened to Piet and what treatment he had received so far. Piet was in and out of unconsciousness and now and then blurt out words that made no sense, like "bugger them all" and "who are the ANC anyway?" Tom knew this was not the end of his short friendship with Piet. He would meet up with that character again one day, somehow.

The Germans were now chattering among themselves and the man in Tom's unit, who said he understood German was continuing on with his translation, whispering what was being said. "They are going to clear out a small tent that houses some bedding supplies and use it for a place to feed us. They want to march us past a couple of hundred troops so they can see what a useless pile of shit we are and how easy it is to defeat us. The Corporal has just caught sight of Rommel marching back towards us, "he looks pissed off".

Rommel, still carrying his serviette and wiping his face had said quietly to the German Sergeant Major "Look here it is quite obvious what your intentions are, but no, sit these POW's down with some dignity and no parading your trophy-captured victims around. Now feed them and get them out of sight. And do it now." Rommel winked at the POW's and marched off, speaking to many of his seated troops on the way back to his table. They all adored him. They would stand up and slap each other's backs and grip forearms or vigorously shake hands. Or Rommel would walk past and tap someone on the head. Tom remembers wondering if he could ever see that happening with a British Commander, perhaps only Churchill.

This instruction had all been in German but the POW's were provided with the translation by Michael Fitzpatrick, a milky white faced lance corporal. Fitzpatrick was from outside Belfast originally, but recently lived in Dagenham, where he had been a loading bay worker at May & Bakers (Manufacturers of, among other items, M&B tablets for Malaria treatment). Tom had selected him originally as he thought he was a Londoner, the same as many of them. Little did he know. The choice worked out well as the translations helped ease their apprehension as they discovered the German army seemed as cocked up as their own.

"Englanders," shouted a guard, "follow me to zis tent and take only one seat for your backside and sit down when you find one." Some chuckles over that instruction lightened up the moment. The tent smelled of mildew and they asked to open the flaps to give them light and fresh air. Then three men brought in a table, some huge pots and a giant five-gallon coffee urn. "No waiters so you help yourself to food and share equal among you." admonished the guard, "I am outside and anyone try to escape I not think but shoot you." This brought on guffaws from everyone.

As if anyone would worry about one guard's presence outside, when trying to escape. "Hmm? Let's see now, how can we get out of here without at least one of the twenty odd thousand troops seeing us?" muttered one young soldier. It was now almost 0800 and the sun had warmed everyone to a nicer comfort level.

They each grabbed a large chunk of pumpernickel, some thin oat porridge and a large piece of cold and very fatty, bratwurst. That food, along with large mugs of hot coffee, seemed to make being a POW quite pleasant; at least for the time being. "Are you thinking it's about time for a nap?" asked one chap, 'Chalky' White, from Welwyn Garden City, "or should we grab the weapons leaning up on that first table over there and simply make a break for it?" "A nap I think and a breakout tomorrow after a good rest," was Tom's response.

Soon they were ordered out of the tent and marched about half a mile to a stockade that contained three wooden huts. They were told these had been built for prisoners of war and they were the first to occupy this stockade. One hut was for ablutions and lavatories, the other two for sleeping quarters. They could use material inside the fence to build another hut if they wanted a dining area. The Germans had heavy equipment and would help with digging foundations and other heavy work.

For two weeks they all worked on building a 12 foot by 16 foot wooden shack and argued with the Germans about metric scale versus the only correct one, theirs. One very short German, weighing about 180 pounds (or was that 82 Kilo's?) was the self-appointed chief engineer.

He was the boss for sure and always argued. "But ve said make ze trench four meters vide," he stormed. But the hapless digger-driver said he went by what the English had drawn on the ground "I follow vot ze British white line says." "Yes," yelled shorty, "but zey don't know zere arse from zere elboos."

Tom remembers, "These were fun filled days. Well as fun as it gets in a POW camp." The two sides clashed over every measurement, but still, one day the project was completed and they made a large table and scrounged folding chairs. They continued to eat sitting on the end of their beds and used this new room to play cards and to scheme and plot. They actually got to use the building for about four days, with very little scheming, when they were informed they were being transferred to Germany by boat and via Italy by train up to a more comfortable and permanent camp. "There you can play with many hundreds of Allied soldiers. So many they have their own football teams. Ve hope you like it," said the Corporal, who was the bum boy belonging to the camp Commandant.

Two months went by before they were told to pack up their personal belongings and place them in individual brown canvas bags, with their names stenciled on it. They each had to sign releases to say they were not mistreated and that they would take care of one wounded POW, Piet Joubert, who had recovered enough to be worthy to travel. At that point, Piet arrived by car and he walked into the room, looking fit and no different from his old self . He had a small bandage on his cheek strapped on with the German equivalent of elastoplast.

"Hey guys, how's it going? Did you miss me?" he smiled. "I've been well looked after by some pretty nice looking nurses. One was named Helmut, another was Anton and my favourite was Willy. I know they liked me as they were fighting daily over who was going to bathe me. Thank Christ that's over".

All of them were marched into a motor pool area and climbed up into a troop carrying truck with four guards. Then they drove off into the desert, which was becoming more hilly and they estimated, in a north west direction. They passed hundreds of burned out or blown up vehicles, mostly allied, from previous unsuccessful battles against Rommel. It took almost two days for them to reach a port somewhere near Benghazi, some Arab name Tom recalls, something like El Gazala. There were a million camels and two ships.

Tom kept a brave face about his present circumstances, but deep down he was scared. Being a prisoner of war would not be easy and this time he felt a sense of doom. He thought he would be locked up and forgotten for many years to come. He did not like where he was and where he was going. He had no control over any of this and simply had to do what he was told to do, by the enemy, and hope he got through it all.

He had no news from England and no real idea of how the war was going. From his point of view it was not going well.

13

JUST ANOTHER SHORT CRUISE

Tom couldn't help feeling that this war was going to last a lot longer than the "pundits" had led people to believe. Even Rommel suggested it would soon be over. And what bothered Tom was it looked very much like the Germans were going to win. Certainly they had superior equipment and manpower. Tom also believed that the Allies manpower were smarter than the Germans, but then again, he knew himself. He kept thinking that if every bloke in the British army was like him, then they didn't stand a chance against Hitler.

Looking at all the wrecked vehicles they had just driven past over the last two days, mostly British vehicles, he was sure the Allies were doomed. While some of his thoughts were justified, based on his limited knowledge and first hand observation, what he couldn't have known was that his timing was just off. Behind all those scenes he had left behind, the Allies were assembling more and more men from all the commonwealth countries. Along with many innovative and much improved British equipment. Tom would have told the boffins back home "When you keep getting blasted by tanks with guns that shoot further and three times more powerful than yours, then build some that can meet and beat those bloody German tanks."

Tom was not able to tell them, but they did it anyway. The equipment being built in England was now based on battle experience, not designed by some planner with World War I expertise. Regretfully, Tom was now out of what was to be a big looming battle, that he would have been proud to be part of (but, deep down, quite relieved that he wasn't).

The Americans had not entered the war and they were badly needed. They had money and enough man-power and equipment to sustain more losses than the Germans. Them coming into the war was exactly what the Allies wanted and needed.

In the early hours of the morning, sometime in mid-July, 1941, a group of twenty disheveled allied soldiers arrived at the seaside in a dusty German truck. At one time it must have been a delightful little beach, but now it was just an oil-stained piece of muddy sand about a mile long. At the end of the strip of muddy sand was an old dock made of stones and concrete, and now extended wider with old railway lines and concrete, built by the Germans to get their equipment ashore.

A German Military Policeman directed the truck to stop at some gates at the edge of the dock. The guards there inspected the truck guards, their papers and every single allied soldier, who were ordered off the truck and then slowly inspected. There was an old, almost empty freighter tied up, around 12,000 tons, that had offloaded some 200 new Panzer tanks and a hundred or so wooden containers filled with spare parts.

The last cargo, oil drums filled with diesel fuel, were being offloaded now. If the Germans were having trouble getting supplies, it certainly did not appear so in this little port. After a few minutes a motorcycle pulled up and the rider got off with a large container of water and some tin mugs that had been in his side car. He told the POW's to drink and if they had to pee, go under the palm trees a few feet away. "When the ship is finished offloading you vill all board and you go to Italy for POW camp, you understand? German luxury just for you," he chortled. He was obviously pleased with himself and his English skills, but also his comedic skills. Nobody else was.

He drove off, with his empty water container and tin mugs, back to the freighter and handed them to a large man in a white jacket standing at the open doors of the ship. Jack Robson, a mate of Tom's, nearly thirty two years old and always kidding around, asked Piet, "You look bloody healthy for a dying man. How the hell are you anyway?"

Piet, now very chirpy, replied, with a big smile "you know I was in Cape Town once and I saw these passenger ships departing for somewhere over the horizon. I thought that one day I could go on such a ship, and take a luxury cruise. And it looks like my dream has come true. Also, I am not even close to dying, so watch your lip in future."

"Yeah," piped up another, "just our bloody luck all the cabin butlers will be on strike!"

A shriek from a whistle on board the German freighter, signaled that the offloading had finished and anyone getting on board should now do so. With that, a couple of German soldiers, trying to look menacing, got the small squad of POW's to march in line toward the gangplank, and enter the bowels of the freighter Feldtmaan, a former Romanian cargo vessel that had been converted into a freighter for Germany. She was also disguised and had quite powerful armaments on board. When no one was looking, this innocent looking vessel would sneak up on Allied shipping and sink them. The Royal Navy did not find this the least bit funny and were eager to get her off the ocean.

As they entered the ship a group of Italian stewards handed each POW a blanket and a bar of soap and then a guard headed them off to the hold, where they would stay until they were to get off, somewhere in Sicily. The ship smelled bloody awful. Oil and diesel fuel, as well as a toilet smell that could not be hidden by the meager attempt to use carbolic or other solutions to take away the odours. Tom said, "It smells like a latrine that just had a thousand Germans 'aving a crap after eating Sauerkraut". Hardly the language used by a proper Englishman but nonetheless, accurately describes the pong."

Piet yelled out, "shoot me now please, or stick pins in my balls. Anything to detract me from this smell. I have never smelled anything so bad and I have been into restaurant toilets in South Africa after eating curry. Almost as bad but it went away after five minutes. This smell seems determined to stick around. And I mean stick!"

Eventually they got to their section of the hold and using whatever junk they could find, they tried to make it comfortable, in spite of the lingering smell. A plank here and a box there, covered with cardboard and news-paper, and soon, a place to sit. Somewhat precarious yes, but a seat. With no portholes they could not see outside but with a lot of engine noise and rumbling below them, they knew they had set sail and would soon be out on the open sea. The journey would be calm across the Mediterranean at most times but at this time of the year especially, very calm.

Most, if not all, the junior staff on board were Italians. There was a noticeable difference in attitude, compared to the Germans attitude. The Germans started the war and they meant to win it. The Italians? Well, not so much. So the POW's found them easier to deal with and managed to scrounge a deck of cards, a few maga-zines, even an Italian newspaper just twelve days old. All of these helped pass the time away. Tom lamented to anyone listening, "If time dragged now, wait until we are all locked up in a permanent POW camp somewhere. How many more months would this war last, and how can we all stand the loneliness as well as the antici-pated hardships?"

So, even though there were card games and the humorous translations of newspapers and Italian maga-zines, what was inside the men's thoughts was far gloom-ier than their outwardly appearance.

"I think I am either growing fond of that shitty smell," one soldier said, "or its actually gone."

"Naaah, it's your bloody nostrils all bunged up and your sense of smell has left you," retorted another.

"Well, I tell you that bloody pair of old pants you are wearing smell like Yorkshire pudding," replied one man obviously looking for an argument to help pass the time.

"You think I am stupid?" was the retort back

"Yeah, alright, I think my brains are better than yours. I bet there is not one puzzle you could catch me on, especially if you thought of the puzzle. Go on, try me. I bet you a quid from my first pay, when we get a first pay that I can solve any puzzle you throw at me".

At that very tense moment two Italian stewards brought in a couple of carts with food and drink on them. "Okay you farty inglesi boys, herea is you lunch break," said a smiley chap and the other piped up, "Anda you very lucky because a you no avva to wash the dishes." For some reason everyone thought this was very funny and the Brits slapped the Italians on the back and smiled at them.

"Jolly dingees," is what one Italian said, "theesa good serveece just today, because you firsta time my guest." The men looked at each other quite bewildered. "What the hell is jolly dingees? " asked one.

"I no say jolly dingees," retorted the Steward, I say 'The only thing is,' but maybe you ear she not so good for listen to Italians with English." Well that had the Brits giggling like schoolgirls, as it dawned on them what was said and what they thought they heard.

"Thank you so veddy bloody much for your service, we appreciate it and have noted your views on the war and your opinion of Hitler," said a Corporal from the crowd, to both Italians. Then everyone started checking out what other food delights were available.

Off walked the two Italians and one said, "I am Luigi Ferranachi and become your visit when war is over to England." Tom remembered thinking that was the last thing he wanted was a visit by an Italian at his place in England. Anyway, it's what people say when they are meeting for the first time.

Lots of bread and tomatoes and cheese, with gallons of water and about a liter each of strong black coffee, was the menu and the men loved it all. They saved about half the water but finished off the rest, slurping it all down and using the backs of their hands and arms to wipe their faces.

Everyone was just nodding off, when up jumped the puzzle man, Martin Shanker, Private, Royal Suffolk Rifles. "Alright smarty pants," he exclaimed, "are you ready, for a one-pound bet?" "This is a simple mathematics quiz. All you have to do is explain it. A fly is flying in a straight line due North, at fifteen feet above the ground. A train is travelling, in the same plane, due south. The fly crashes into the train and dies in a mushy heap, on the front of the train. Immediately, the fly changes direction, from due north to due south. Okay, got the picture?" He beamed over at Lance Corporal William Hanglin.

"Yeah, I got the picture now hurry up with the question," said Hanglin.

"Right, well just before it changed direction, for a billionth of a second, the fly actually stopped moving.... north, stop, then south. Do you agree?"

"Yes, it stopped motion," replied Hanglin.

"And where was the fly when it stopped motion?" asked Shanker.

"Well, stuck to the bleedin' train, wasn't it" confirmed Hanglin.

"So, I'm glad you said that, cos, I'm getting to the answer now, if the fly stopped motion and it stopped while it was stuck to the train, then the train must have stopped as well, right?"

Well, this silly story got the whole bunch of them arguing as to whether it was possible. Where was Pythagoras when you needed him? What would Einstein say about it? Needless to say, it really passed the time. The entire afternoon flew by and nobody of course, could answer the stupid conundrum. The bet became a non-issue and everyone agreed it was a great way to get everyone to get a little adrenalin into their systems.

Piet said, excitedly, "Okay, I've got one for you, how's this for a great puzzle? There's two blokes in a compartment together on a train in South Africa, with nothing to do. One guy was English and the other a jaapie, like me, eh. The Englishman says, 'Let's play a game where one bloke tells a story, and the other has to guess what book he is talking about okay? Here is the first puzzle. I have a valley. It's a very green valley, what's the name of the book?"

"The Afrikaaner says, "Geesh man I have no idea.""

The Englishman responds: "well, of course, the book is 'how green was my Valley."

"Oh jaah now I get it," says the Afrikaaner, slapping his forehead, "now it's my turn. This Boer was driving his 1932 Ford Lorry on a dirt road and suddenly he got a flat tire. But when he looked in the toolbox for a jack, he realized he had forgotten it at home. He thought maybe he could push some chewing gum in the hole in the tire and then pump it up with just enough air that he could drive to the nearest garage. So he pumps the hand pump up and down for ten minutes and finally rushes into the cab, starts the lorry and drives off, leaving the pump in the middle of the road. Five minutes later another lorry ran over the pump. So what's the name of the book?"

"Well I have absolutely no bloody idea, my man," harrumphs the Englishman, "what is it?"

Piet looked around and asked his fellow POW's, "Okay, does any of you know?" Everyone looked stunned and they all vigorously shook their heads. "Okay," says Piet, "the Afrikaaner says, "The book is called, 'The last days of pump eh."

Piet doubled up with laughter, holding the stitches still in his jaw, little laughter from other sources, just groans. It was now about 1500 and their day had gone about as well, under the circumstances, as it could go. Piet was wandering around explaining his joke. "You see with a stronger accent than mine, pump sounds like pomp, so when he said"…… .

"Yes Piet, we get it," they said, cutting him off, but not mean spiritedly.

At that moment the Feldtmaan's Captain, Walter Haigler, a skinny man about six foot tall with terrible razor burn, or a skin rash, wrapped around his lower face, he entered with two junior officers, both carved out of Hitler's desired dream of tall, blond and blue eyed Gods. Haigler snapped his heels together then straightened his cap and began addressing the POW's. "Gentlemen, you are all a big nuisance. My job is easy" said the Captain, in quite good English. "When I just have freight to carry. But human freight is not so good, and when that freight is enemy prisoners, like you, I want to get you off my ship quickly. We can only feed you what we have available, so no complaints please.

I understand one of you is injured and we wish to get him examined by our doctor on board, right now. That man, get up and go with Sub Lt. Schmidt to the upper deck. You will be back in two hours or less, unless the doctor wants to experiment on you; heh! heh!" With that Piet was escorted out and the Captain continued. "We shall only be another day and you will then be dropped off in Sicily where we have many other POW's from North Africa, at least 45,000, so maybe some old chaps you used to know and you can play with each other, until the end of this war. Don't expect the war to end that soon, but certainly by the summer of '43. I must go about my duties now. If you have any important questions ask them now." Nobody had, so he left.

Some men slept, others played Whiskey Poker and some just lay on the floor and counted the rivets in the ceiling. If some had not had on a wristwatch, they would not know the time. There was no way they could know when the sun was going down or coming up. Someone said it was 1550 so they knew dinner would be sooner than later. An hour later they were brought shredded chicken and some macaroni in a tomato sauce. They were also given two iceberg lettuces and a big plain sponge cake, along with coffee.

Eventually all the men had washed and tried to clean their teeth and after attempting a few more silly jokes and waiting for Piet to get back, they dozed off and slept soundly throughout the night. Piet had been operated on, with a local anesthetic and was now feeling quite a bit more comfortable. The previous German Doctor, in Rommel's camp, had tied the stitches too tight and they had been adjusted, as well as a little dentistry alignment performed. Ironically, the Doctor had trained in South Africa in the early 1930's at the Groote Schuur Hospital in Cape Town, so he and Piet ended up chatting a lot. Piet was told of the small operation and that he may have to have a liquid diet for a few days afterwards. The doctor arranged for Piet to have a cream of chicken soup and a sandwich of ham and lettuce prior to the op. They spent an hour talking, as the doctor really had no other patients to tend to.

The two men liked each other and the doctor particularly hated Hitler. As he was an upper class member of the intelligencia, which most German fighting forces were not, his type were not usually respected in wartime Germany. Of course he asked Piet not to repeat his feelings or he could be sent to a slave camp and he rather liked the back and forth boat ride, he had been on for over a year.

Feeling dirty and stiff from sleeping on hard surfaces, even the lucky ones who had cardboard or newspaper to lie on, the rag-tag bunch of POW's awoke at various times between 0600 and 0800. Bored to tears and uncomfortable as hell, they all tried their own ways to wake and become alive. They were not that fit anymore so there was very little jumping-jacks. Here and there were arms swinging over the head, and a few feeble attempts at touching toes. Eventually they could probably form a squad and march around, if push came to shove. At 0830 the same two Italian stewards arrived with some German garlic sausage and lots of white bread, and lots of coffee. The men devoured it in minutes. They had not lost their appetite. Piet had lots of coffee.

14

A CHANGE IN CRUISE SHIPS

After about ten minutes, the German doctor came down carrying a chocolate oatmeal banana hot drink, sweetened with honey. "I do apologize Piet, but they forgot your breakfast drink. Also, before you drink it I want to examine your jaw." He prodded and peered and then said, "everything looks fine but stick to liquids for about a week." With that, he left. Piet swallowed the liter or so of the drink and gave it a thumbs up.

"Just a whole day we need to kill now," said Tom rather glumly, when suddenly the ship keeled over to starboard and sirens began clanging, as well as whooping. Loudspeakers announced: "Achtung achtung, aufmerksamkei, die wir sindunder beschuss von meer. Alle stationen kampfen". (attention we are under attack by sea, man your stations) Chuck McGrall yelled out, "We are under attack, get ready to exit here quickly. Get your shoes on and any belongings you simply must keep and get ready".

The German doctor said, "Get out of the hold and get on deck, we have been hit by a British ship". All the men ran up the long flight of steps and almost as soon as they had reached a deck where they could see what was going on, the ship started sliding to starboard. Seawater started pouring into the hold where all of the POW's had been moments before.

The Captain yelled down from the bridge "abandon ship, zum verlassen des schiffes". "All English jump over now. Save yourselves, we are no longer responsible". Yelled the Captain, using the ships loudspeaker system.

The ship yawed and then screamed as metal surrendered to the sea. Jagged edges of metal, where a torpedo had entered the prow, were ripping apart and water was now unstoppable from filling the entire ship. Now the Germans and Italians were floundering in the water together, which had now reached the bridge level and, as the two funnels snapped off the Feldtmaan skidded into a death spiral. Everyone heaved themselves away from the doomed vessel as fast as they could. At least sixty men were in the sea, and now another forty or fifty joined them.

The sea had become a muddy froth of diesel fuel and then goopy black oil started rising to the surface. Tom saw one of the Italian stewards seemingly unable to stop drinking in a lot of oil and he saw him go under. There was little Tom could do but watch him disappear. Tom remembered from the last time this happened that timing was important when breathing and staying above the oil slick. He watched waves carefully, and like a surfboarder looking for a high wave, he got pushed to the top of a wave, almost jumped out of the wave and then took a deep breath. At least he was not taking in Oil and Fuel, and hardly any sea water. This went on for what seemed like hours but was about forty minutes. The number of men visible in the water decreased as each victim surrendered to the peacefulness of simply giving in. Feedback from other incidents like this suggests there is apparently some peace in just letting one's head go back and simply lie down. Just a few seconds and all your misery and pain has left you. But not for Tom. He was an experienced "sinking ship person". He had done this before and he knew help was on its way. And then, there it was, a destroyer from the Royal Navy, "de ja vous all over again," thought Tom. "Same bloody circumstances".

Then, from the deck of the destroyer a megaphone blared out, "We have a rope ladder on either side of our ship. Swim up to it and time your grip with a wave. You don't want to rip your arms out of your sockets. Move up with a wave and grab the ropes. Plant your feet on the rungs and then wait for the next swell to help you up the rope." Another sailor yelled out, "Use the life belts we are throwing down, save your energy, slip the belt over your arms. Arms up through the belt then swim to the ship. "Schwimmen auf das Schiff und klettern die seile" (swim toward our ship and climb the ropes" one RN sailor yelled through a megaphone, in perfect German). Amidst all the yelling and moaning and watching the Feldtmaan sink, unfortunately sucking a dozen or so men down with her, some men had reached the rope netting and were now climbing up. Some had made it to safety and were now on board.

Tom was now a yard or so from the rope mesh and he watched the swells. He watched and timed the pattern of the sea against the ship, and then he lunged forward and had a hold of the ropes. Then his feet found the right footholds below him and he was secure. Of course now he could get smashed to death against the sides of the ship as the ropes banged each time a wave hit. However, bit by bit, Tom was able to heave himself up, one rung at a time. He had maybe fifteen more rungs to go. One of the British sailors peered over the deck ready to give a helping hand to the next man, when he looked straight into Tom's face, some five feet below, swaying on the rope netting and in a loud Cockney voice yelled, "'ere you, if you like our bleedin boat so much why don't you buy a bleedin ticket"?

Tom looked up and recognized a sailor who he had met on the ship that rescued him about a year ago. Indeed this destroyer was the very same ship, HMS Tynedale and of course most of her crew would likely be the same as well. Somehow this news helped Tom suddenly find new strength. Soon he was crossing over the wooden rail of the deck and collapsing in the arms of the familiar sailor.

"Come on matey, stand up, let's have a look at you. Come over 'ere and take all these rotten clothes off. Who gave you these anyway, the British Army or the bloody Germans? Let's find you a nice Royal Navy jumpsuit and later on we shall find you a vest and some underwear. Now stand there and soap yourself down everywhere and

I will direct the "hosepipe". Tom remembers thinking how sweet the smell was of carbolic soap and how wonderful it was to use whatever solvent he was given to get all lubricants out of his hair. The first navy blue jumpsuit he was given fitted him perfectly. He zipped it up and felt very comfortable in the warm serge. It was exactly the same suit Winston Churchill wore when he was aboard a Royal Navy ship, but perhaps a wee bit smaller.

Then he was given some sort of mouthwash that tasted like a mixture of schoolboy glue and concentrated peppermint toothpaste. He had to mix it with water to thin it out, then told to gargle, rinse and spit it out into a drain. Tom started to giggle as he watched the faces of the other men doing the same thing, he said, "All of us look like we have been ordered to suck a lemon dipped in goose shit." Still, they all squirmed and pulled faces and closed their eyes, as if that would ease the dreadful taste, and did what they were told, like good little boys.

The weather was warm so Tom was soon dry and using the towel to dry off completely, he was sent inside, introduced to a medic at a table armed with huge hypodermic syringes. "Anti-biotics, tetanus and flu," said the medic, jab, jab, jab. "Sit down over there and someone will interview you and get details. There will be one shot of Rum and you can have it in Cocoa or straight". Tom had his Rum straight and then had a hot cocoa "Hmmm, could I have some Rum in my cocoa?" asked Tom.

"It's already got some in it," said the steward.

"'Ere, smell it, taste it, now has that got any rum in it?' pleaded Tom.

"Sorry about that, musta missed it, "said the steward, pouring rum into Tom's cocoa. "'ere 'ave a little extra on the 'ouse". Tom smiled, "Thank you, my son, you will be rewarded in heaven."

The smooth warm silken drink worked better than any of those other shots in the arm Tom had that day. For the first time he felt safe and in good hands, but a little concerned about where to next.

The Axis crew were all hosed down, given any medical aid they might have needed, and given three jabs of medicine. No different treatment for them; they even got a shot of rum in a hot cocoa. They were given white jump suits, and marched down to the quarters that had been sealed off for them. They were placed in a forward officers meeting room and part of an unused cafeteria. Some eighty crew were to be housed there until they could be delivered on shore somewhere safe. It was believed thirty-five Axis crew had been lost at sea, including the Captain, who appeared to purposely go down with his ship.

Tom took a stroll along the deck of the Tynedale, although the Captain had warned that a Luftwaffe attack, that close to Crete, could be imminent and if that happened all would be back below. The RAF, however, had recently become the masters of the sky above the Mediterranean, so few Luftwaffe aircraft were about to fly up for a challenge. At that moment eight RAF Hurricanes flew over the Tynedale at about 200 feet. With a waggle of wings and a roar to get height, the pilots shoved forward their throttle, right above the ship and climbed up until they disappeared in the clouds, about seven thousand feet above. What a welcome sight and what a welcoming ceremony. Some Germans still on the deck applauded the R.A.F. This was much to the chagrin of the "die-hard" nazi officers who, no doubt would be taking notes and reporting back to the "officials" when they got home. After the air-show everyone slowly trickled back inside to their quarters.

About half the men, on both sides, while physically okay, were still retching and spewing out the remainder of whatever combination they had swallowed while swimming before rescue. Many were very weak and had to stay in cots arranged in rows on the cafeteria floor. Even so, in spite of the horrible event, there were no signs of anyone now on board Tynedale facing loss of life.

Tom found Piet, sitting on a stairwell, just below the bridge, sharing a cigarette break with a Lieutenant Commander who said he was "twenty-eight years old, joined the navy in 1938, and loved every minute of it, especially sinking enemy ships. We sank eight this year but this one this morning was only the second we sank that had POW's on it. One of my chaps tells me that there is one of you lot that was actually on the first one we sank about a year ago. Astounding."

"Good afternoon, Sir," said Tom, extending his hand. "I am Tom Gale and I was on board the German ship, Tanganyika, which you sank last year near Emdem. I am extremely pleased to meet you, but then, today I am extremely pleased to meet anyone".

"My God," replied The Lt. Commander, "can you understand what the odds are for that to happen? If there was a lottery today I would urge you to buy a ticket. And how did you meet this rascal South African?"

"Well, that's easy, I was ordered to find twenty-one men for a tactical squad to fight Rommel with fast moving half-tracks against his almighty Panzer tanks. I found twenty but needed one more and in desperation I chose Piet. He sort of turned out okay, I suppose. Although he tells the most awful jokes, right Piet?"

"So this bloke walks into a bar in Pretoria," says Piet, "and orders a beer. A monkey was playing on the roof rafters and immediately swung down and pissed in the guy's beer. Furious he called the barman over and says 'your bloody monkey peed in my beer'. The barman says, "no man that monkey belongs to the piano player. Go sort it out with him". So the guy walks over and yells at the piano player. 'Do you know your monkey peed in my beer?" The piano player replies, "No, but hum a few bars and I'll see if I can pick it up."

" Hmmm! I see what you mean, says the Lt. Commander. "Look here, I have to get back to the bridge. Come upstairs to our quarters, just the two of you, at about 1800, and enjoy a meal with some of us. Don't say anything, you know, NCO's and officers et al. Understand? I am Alex Coulthard, by the way, from Watford, Hertfordshire."

"Well, we would be delighted," says Piet, "in spite of Watford. See you at six. Cheers, eh."

Piet and Tom strolled along the deck like the two friends they had become, just chatting about life in general and plans for the future. Piet puts his arm around Tom and says, "Look Tom, this war won't last forever. I have a huge farm in the free-state back in South Africa and I am always looking for people to help me run it. Please come and stay with me for a month as soon as the war ends. If you like what you see we can fix you up with a job. I need all kinds of people from accounting, to construction or even chasing rhino's. Promise me you'll come."

"I promise I will be there," said Tom, quite excitedly, "because if I have nothing to do after the war, I will end up robbing banks, or attacking little old Ladies, for their tea money."

The Tynedale now had an arduous task of by-passing German U-Boats patrolling the Mediterranean and getting to a friendly port to off-load all POW's and Army personnel. The Germans had lost command of the seas but were still a threat. The Allies were told that they were heading for Gibraltar where they could catch a plane and fly to England. The Germans would be transported to Spain and handed over there.

A DC3 would be able to take all Allied prisoners in one flight; it would be the best and likely the safest way to get them all home. A day-and-a-half later the Tynedale sailed into Gibraltar. The Allied troops were disembarked first and, with no ceremony, were marched to a large bus and were whisked off to the airport. Then the Germans were all marched off the ship, with three on stretchers with non life-threatening medical issues. All were placed into three buses and driven to the border with Spain. The Tynedale refueled and took on supplies then departed very quickly to continue patrol of the Mediterranean Sea close to Malta and where possible, prevent Germans in North Africa from being re-supplied from Italy.

15

NEW DIRECTIONS FOR TOM

The troops bounced about as they were whisked across the tarmac of the airport. At the far end of the airfield sat a camouflaged DC3, with RCAF markings, a Canadian troop carrier on loan for that troop transfer. The men all jumped out of the truck and climbed four steps into the aircraft, which had a centre aisle and quite comfortable seats. Forty-eight seats were available and everyone grabbed the seat that they preferred. Within half an hour they were flying north west towards Plymouth, which took them four hours. The plane landed on a grass runway and came to a halt near some hangars, as far away from the terminal building as possible, and they were all marched in by some Warrant Officer and all were told to rest up on some cots, until their name was called for de-briefing. Tom found a cot he liked and within minutes was fast asleep. Perhaps two hours went by before his name was called. He then was asked a lot of serious questions, ranging from the type of armament on board the German ship, to the demeanor of the typical German soldier in the desert. Tom gave them answers and was then told to wait, back on his cot, if he wished, as someone was coming to pick him up.

Tom waited about an hour, fell asleep and then tossed and turned until he heard his name called. "Gale" yelled a 2nd Lieutenant, "show yourself. 1 am Clarkson and I have to escort you to the Captain's office. You must be a VIP otherwise they would have me marching you over there. It's only about 12 miles. Never mind we have a lovely car on loan from the Navy, a Wolseley, and you get to sit in it. Okay? Let's go through these doors and quick march. Left, left, left, right, left. Here we are, this green one. You can sit up front with me. Shove your kit…hey, where is your kit, Gale?"

"I am wearing it. Hidden under this jump suit I am hiding underpants and a vest. In the left pocket is a toothbrush and in the right pocket is half a Mars bar. And, Sir, that is my total kit. I suppose you heard that we were prisoners on a gerry ship that the navy sunk? Because my other kit is somewhere near Malta in 100 fathoms of water," explained Tom, quite slowly and dripping with sarcasm.

"Oh Shit," said the officer, "I never knew. But look, let's do something about that shall we. I will take you over to see Sergeant Major Hodgkins who is the Army quartermaster for this outfit. He will fit you out with army stuff and a few extras. Alright, Gale?" Tom murmured agreement.

"Sergeant Gale, hmmm, you are a size 40. Waist 36, inside leg 32, and collar 15. Am I right?" beamed the QM, when they reached the huge warehouse with every style and size of Army gear as was available. "And shoes 11?"

"Pretty close," retorted Tom, "Waist 32, inside leg 32 and collar 15, shoes 12. But I promised a decent sailor that I would keep his navy jump suit forever, so I won't wear it but I must keep it. Let me get back to my beloved Army kit," Tom said at the time he could care less about army kit but he thought that buttering up the QM may just mean a better edition battle-dress jacket. One that was smoother and warmer, and with better quality trousers and shoes. He was right.

As if he was in Saville-Row, where all the richest blokes and military officers get their made-to-measure be-spoke suits made, Tom was being treated like one, by the QM. "Wait a mo, that jacket is a smidge too big. Let me try a newer brand that we just got in, made in India out of 100% cotton and much finer tailoring than the gypo ones we were using. The Indians seem to take more pride in their work. Aah now that's much better, and the trousers will fit as well. Get that bloody navy suit out of my sight. Sit on it over here and try on these black shoes. 12 narrow fit, calf leather, made in Scotland. There ya go, like a bleedin brothel creeper. Right Corporal, get me two of everything here as well as two Egyptian cotton white shirts, 15 collar 32 sleeves. And what Regiment tie do you want Gale?" The QM asked, "we have all of them here".

"I suppose it's too late to ask for the Buckingham Palace Dragoons?' asked Tom with a wink, "so I suppose it's the King's Rifles, then."

With that Tom was given all his ablution kit, such as soap, toothpaste a toothbrush, two shoe brushes a spare tie "Just in case you slop gravy all over one of them," admonished the QM.

Carrying a new kitbag and wearing his new army gear, along with a friendly piece of advice from the QM, "keep this to yourself, Gale, but those socks are 100% wool and only officers get them, isn't that right, Sir?" the QM said, addressing the only officer in the room, 2nd Lt. Clarkson, "and I suppose you want a couple of extras yourself so I can buy your silence?" Clarkson agreed.

Tom felt pretty good and pretty smart when he got back into the car headed for the Captain's office. Ten minutes later he was marched into the Captain's office and there was Colonel Dowdall. "Tom, I have been waiting to see you. Somehow we eluded gerry and I was able to track back to Algiers and flew home last week. I understand you were sunk by our chaps in the Med. Is that right? It's so bloody nice to see you again. We must have dinner and swap stories. How about tonight, here, with me and Brig. General Farrell, he has something in mind for you".

"Not the bloody desert again? Moaned Tom. "And yes it is so good to see you, Sir" and the two men actually hugged. This was not a WWII practice among Englishmen, especially military men and even more so the difference in rank, but they hugged anyway. " Dinner, yes, please," responded Tom.

"Now, before we go any further, this is Captain Willman, as he swung around to introduce the 30 ish year old sturdy young officer, and he is the one man you must treat kindly. He is responsible for all your pay, health benefits, insurance and pension," said Dowdall. And then beaming, as if Tom was his son, stood up and said "Captain, may I introduce you to my good friend and fine soldier, and very capable Sergeant, Tom Gale, of the King's Rifles."

Tom stood upright snapped his heels and gave the Captain a salute and then as the Captain responded, they shook hands firmly. "I've heard quite a bit about you, Tom, and I am pleased to know you. I shall be at that dinner tonight, if you wish to change your mind, ha! ha!"

Tom seemed to feel very comfortable among these officers and wondered why they were so nice to him. Then a very large man entered the room from a back office. He was possibly 6 feet 3 or 4 inches tall, shoulders like a rugby player, wearing jodhpurs and braces with no jacket. His hair was blonde and he had a large gunslinger moustache, and every finger was stained with nicotine. He had a large cigar in his right hand and his clear brown eyes sparkled as he boomed out, "Gentleman please be seated, aah! this must be Gale. Pleased to meet you Gale, at ease, no formalities today, just friends discussing events, past and planned. I am Brigadier General Farrell, at one time, head of the Transvaal Cavalry in South Africa. Downing Street brought me over here to be right-hand-man for General Smuts. I met Smuts on my first day in England, in December 1939, and I haven't

145

seen him since. Har har de har." With a very loud guffaw, he bent over spluttering and spitting into a wastebasket. "So now I am behind the scenes making up stories to impress the troops, surprise the enemy and keep the populace calm. It's a bit like playing rugby in South Africa. You have to show off your past record when it's good, to intimidate the team you are playing against next weekend, then fake injuries to your finest players, and then roll up on play day with all your team present and beat the pulp out of the enemy.

Okay, look here, Gale, we can chat and tell lies at dinner tonight, my quarters, just the four of us and say about 1900. Is that Okay for everyone? Fits your plans Dowdall, Clarkson?" They both nodded, "Alright, must bugger off now and create some lies. Gale, I might just pick your devious mind at dinner. Maybe a Sergeant with your battleground experience, and I hear also Navy background, might have some interesting ideas? Until tonight then, oh, by the way, anyone love Broccoli, 'cos I have taken it off the menu tonight, I hate the damn stuff and if anyone here wants it, come back tomorrow." Then Farrell turned and marched out of the room, swishing a pile of papers off the desk, no doubt caused by the vacuum he created when his large mass was suddenly not there.

Tom asked if he could go for a walk, down to a park he had seen earlier while being driven over to just sit and have a smoke and get his head clear. Just be on his own for a while. Everyone thought that was a terrific idea as they had work to do, so all agreed to meet at 1830 back in Captain Clarkson's office. Tom sat on a bench, watching mothers and children, playing and gossiping and doing what they always do: live life. He got very distraught over what men were doing to each other in the sea and in the desert so that life such as this could continue. He could not get into his head why Hitler would do what he was doing to improve the life of his people, when, even if he won, their lives would be worse than they were before the war started. And why kill all those Jews? He looked across the street at about thirty men waiting for a bus. He wondered how many were Jews, and what differences there would be if ten were Catholics and ten were Jews and ten were Germans. Who could tell the difference and so what if one could? He got angry and decided to slowly walk back, the long way round, to reach the Captain's office at the required 1830. He calmed down a bit as he walked and was there at 1830.

All the men went into a small dining room which could hold maybe ten diners at once, so the four of them had lots of room. Brig. Gen Farrell's steward brought in Mulligatawny Soup as a starter, along with lumpy brown dinner rolls and margarine. Then a steak and kidney pie, brimming with onion, carrots, steak and, of course kidney, steaming hot and all in a rich gravy. The pie was big enough for maybe eight or nine guests. "Eat up, lads," said Farrell, "there's more coming". Then a platter of mashed potatoes and an enormous bowl of baked beans, with roasted parsnips on another plate. Then the steward sidled out into the kitchen and left the four men to themselves.

"First things first," announced Dowdall. "Tom, we cannot believe what you have been through since April last year. Also, we do not think the Army has treated you well or even used you well. So, we want you to stick around here for a few months and help us with some plans we have for the troops in battle. Your experience will help us a lot. It is now nearly July and we need you here for a while.

Then, in December, we propose and assume you will accept, that we send you on an ocean cruise. You and two men from your original Calais outfit, who you can choose, will sail from Southampton to Cape Town, on a Union-Castle liner, and you will have a job to do for us." Farrell says "This was my idea but I had not known about you, so when discussing it with Col. Dowdall, he mentioned you."

"Yes," said Dowdall, "and Captain Clarkson here is the right chap to take all the little bits and put them into one file, quickly and accurately, so that is why he's involved".

Tom felt very good about this and beamed. "Look gentlemen, let me tell you the cruise idea is a good one and maybe I can complete the trip this time. The last two cruises were interrupted by the bleedin Royal Navy. But what about this job, then? What is it you want me to do?"

"Let me explain why the cruise to South Africa," interrupted Farrell. "Firstly, anyone need another beer? Now that is an important decision. Arthur," he yelled out to the steward, "bring in four more beers please, Double Diamond is Okay. Secondly, I had been in a meeting with Lord Beaverbrook making a presentation a month or so ago. The gist of his speech was that we had cooperation from all countries in the Empire, but, other than allowing troops to help the Allied cause, South Africa was not contributing to the war effort. I know that South Africa is a very wealthy country, blessed with rich agricultural land to grow food. A lot of large tracts of forest to supply much needed lumber and many valuable minerals to help manufacture war material. Plus a lot of labour forces. Beaverbrook wanted to know a way to persuade the Government of South Africa to be more sympathetic to the Allies cause, and start providing anything they could to help us. Furniture, canned soups, meats, fish and vegetables. Cannon shells, bullets, pillows, sheets, army uniforms; all these would help their economy grow and set them up for more and better business after the war, and so on.

Someone suggested we have films distributed to every little town and show how bad the war was and how the world would be affected if Germany won. I thought it would be better if it were more personal and have a real person with some good stories about his own battle experiences and how the troops were crying out for supplies. That's where Colonel Dowdall thought of you, Tom."

Col. Dowdall stepped in. "You see Tom, you may not realize this, but you do have some great stories to tell, and the South African people are not opposed to the war, but rather, appear indifferent. As you know, at first there was an objection to help England against anyone, after they were treated so badly during the Boer War at the turn of the century. Times have changed, but still, the war is not a daily topic and unless someone has a child or other relative overseas fighting in the war, they rarely think of it. So, Tom, you are that relative. You can represent that person's son as you tell your stories.

You can tell them on board the ship and you can tell them at a venue in Cape Town and then we fly you to Johannesburg where we can arrange a venue there. Fly you back to Cape Town, spend a few days relaxing, and a speech here and there, depending on the demand, mostly from military sources I should imagine. After that, catch another ship sailing back to Southampton, about five days later."

"So how does that seem to you, Tom?" asked Captain Clarkson.

"Well, I am not a trained speaker but I have been known to tell a few stories, and if someone will help me with what to say, and what to leave out, I'll do it," replied Tom. "Now then I need another beer and another sclunge of that steak and kidney Pie, and a scoop of those beans." The evening went well. Everyone was jolly; possibly six or seven beers each might just be the cause of the merriment? They all went their separate ways after dinner. Captain Clarkson arranging to meet one more time to hand over all the paperwork, (tickets, itineraries, South African cash, speeches, etc) and then the meeting was over.

16

A REWARD ON A REAL CRUISE SHIP

The Stirling Castle was the ship. A beautiful lilac and white, 22,000 ton passenger ship owned by Union-Castle line. The sailing date was December 12, 1941, and Tom's Trio, as Dowdall liked to refer to them, had been recruited and taken to class almost daily, for the past few weeks days or so, and sworn to secrecy. They were given notes on emphasizing words, and put through role-plays, for answering questions of the press and the public.

They were briefed on the politics of South Africa and advised not to become embroiled in any matters involving Dutch and English points of view and to not fraternize with any indigenous natives. "And don't get drunk, you are flying the flag for England," warned Dowdall, with a wink. Then they were ready to go.

On a surprisingly warm and calm night with clear skies and calm seas, along with 59 F weather, the Stirling Castle set sail from Southampton, with her first stop in Funchal, a Portuguese territory in the Canary Islands, some four days away. Tom had asked if he could have Piet Joubert with him, but, because he was South African, the Boffins thought it would not help the message they wanted three English boys to get across.

Eventually the other two selected were Fred Pawson, a skinny thirty-two year old, with very little hair left. He was from Birmingham. The other was John Haskins, a tall, skinny, blonde thirty-two year old from Clacton-on-Sea. Tom was the youngest at twenty-six. He explained after that the three of them had as much in common as a "Tonga tribesman, a Welsh coalminer and a Mongolian Yak Shepherd." But they had been close from the first episode in Calais and got closer on this cruise. They took their job seriously and they played a form of quiz during the day, testing each other and listening to not just the right answers, but also the manner in which the response was given.

Of course they did all their rehearsal work in any of the fine lounges on board, or out on the sunny decks, near the giant funnels and away from the wind. They certainly did not want sensitive papers blowing into the Indian Ocean and into the hands of an enemy.

They also noted that there were a lot of nurses on board, just graduated from college, on their way to career opportunities in Africa. All three men felt it their duty to help these young ladies learn all about Africa, as they had been there themselves, thus had experiences the nurses could use to make their assimilation so much easier. They explained this to the ladies as they bought them drinks, mostly beer shandies, and told them they were always available to help. The ladies giggled and joined the men and so the education began. John explained how the Zulu tribe was formed and how Chaka, the Zulu Chief, treated women and signs to watch for. Fred explained the Chipongwe tribes theory on religion, while Tom was the expert on civil laws and how the different tribes reacted to White Settlers in The Orange Free State compared to the Belgian Congo.

All of this knowledge was astounding as these three men had only been to North Africa, where Arabs lived. They had never been to any of the countries they were pontificating on. There was and never has been, a Chipongwe tribe, and as for civil law in either the Congo or the free state, well?

It was fun and the Nurses knew it was all BS, but the men were charming and reasonably good looking, and everyone was an adult, so they all had 15 days at sea, learning a little and drinking a lot, and never bored in the evenings. They had a smooth sail and an uneventful stop at the Canary Islands.

Christmas was a jolly affair. The lads and the nurses exchanged little gifts but lots of smudged lipstick. The Captain, dressed as Santa, handed each man a gift of a Ronson cigarette lighter, with an engraved picture of the Stirling Castle Ship on it. The ladies got compacts, similarly engraved. Stuffed with roast beef, yorkshire Pudding, turkey and all the trimmings, plus a rich

Christmas pudding soaked in rum, they then assembled on the main deck.

With a cool breeze flowing across the ship and the moonlight glistening on the Indian Ocean, they watched a film with Bob Hope and Bing Crosby, in "The Road to Morocco". All three men thought Dorothy Lamour, not the star of the show, deserved all the whistles she got. A screen was rolled down and a 16 MM projector with four reel changes provided the state-of-the-art technology for an almost flicker free movie. Cigarette smoke wafted up lazily and many dozed off during the film.

17

IS THIS ON THE SAME PLANET?

On a cool December 27 , the Sterling Castle docked in Cape Town. The journey had passed without any issues. Where this part of the world used to be patrolled heavily by German U-Boats, they were all now required in the Mediterranean, as their numbers had reduced dramatically. Now and then an Avro Shackleton, submarine spotter airplane, of The South African Air force, would fly low over the ship, waggling its wings. "Those bastards," yelled Paul jokingly, shaking his fist at the plane "they are just showing off for the nurses, so they can meet them in Cape Town".

The trio arrived in Cape Town and were taken to the Cullinan Hotel on the waterfront and each given a room. This really was a magnificent hotel and they were very impressed.

Tom recalls, " I don't know if Captain Clarkson or General Farrell arranged this, but I wonder if they know there are less expensive hotels here?" This was beyond anything they had ever seen, let alone be living in. A quick press conference was held for the three soldiers, halfway up Devil's Peak Mountain. There were some other unknown British soldiers also touring Cape Town. They were there for a short three day rest and were on a convoy leading to India. They all teamed up for the day and had a few beers, and "shot the shit" as the army says, discovering which battles each had experienced. It seems the other blokes had been part of the Dunkirk escape. They paid for every beer when they discovered that Fred, John and Tom, had helped them by their bravado in Calais.

The City Mayor's representative said, "Look, you must be tired from your trip and you are not needed for your presentation until Saturday night, right here in the main ballroom, so rest up. I have a driver reserved for you and a big Chevrolet limousine. He will show you around Cape Town, as you wish. Ask the front desk to get him when you need him and he will be in the car waiting for you at the front entrance. Use him as you wish but remember he has a home to go to so, if you plan on staying out beyond ten p.m., then let him go home and give him twelve hours before you use him again. Use a taxi if you are dilly-daddling at some night club, or somewhere else, if you know what I mean.

By the way I am Alan Buurstein, and my phone number is on my card. You just dial nine from your room phone and then my number. If you are in any trouble or have questions, just call. I will want to talk to you in the ballroom, around three p.m. on Saturday. See you then."

"Geesh," exclaimed John, after Alan had left the room, "it's Thursday and we have a car, a driver and two nights to kill. Do you think we could get up to any trouble by Saturday? I also hear that the local girls are very interested in learning proper English as they only speak Afrikaans at home and at their jobs. As we speak the King's English, proper like, then maybe we could find some willing students somewhere; huh, whatcha think eh?"

Tom, being in charge said, "Yes, but as long as we do not embarrass the British Empire and Brigadier General Farrell."

18

THE PRICE OF THE CRUISE

Saturday night arrived quickly. The trio had been exemplary tourists. They had used Tulele, their Cape Malay chauffeur to the fullest. They had gone to the top of Table Mountain, seen the Botanical Gardens, visited Clifton Beach and got a little sunburned. They drove to Fischoek, a nearby fishing village and then walked around the city and up and down Adderley Street.

They phoned every hotel in the book and every hospital, trying to find those nurses, but sadly, they did not know that those girls had all boarded a train, on the same day they arrived, and were headed for Salisbury, Southern Rhodesia, as landed immigrants and full time staff at various hospitals in that country. C'est la vie. Tulele volunteered some girls he knew in a large house, downtown. The men declined. The bars were seemingly for men only and no girls were to be found anywhere.

The first presentation was happening right then. The Mayor had sent out word to his cronies who, in turn, had sent the message around that this was a war effort and no other city would beat Cape Town's efforts to contribute in some fashion. The Mayor, Willem Geldenhuys, stood proudly at the lectern. "We are here tonight," he said, sounding much like a member of the British Royal family, "enjoying fine Cape wine and local Kingklip fish. For you British, king clip is to us like the finest salmon from Canada. Enjoy this magnificent meal and brag about it when you get home. But at the very north of this same continent, our boys are fighting, and dying, to maintain our freedom of religion and lifestyle.

In concert with Downing Street, in London, I have arranged for some British troops, who have actually been in battle, against the Germans, to tell you how you can help them. Please give a warm welcome to Sergeant Thomas Gale, of the Royal Rifles."

Tom stood up from the nearby table, and wiped his mouth with a serviette and walked up two stairs to the lectern. There were only about 400 people in the cavernous ballroom, but they were the cream of the Cape's upper class. They were all white. They had between them about 90% of all the wealth in the Cape Province. Tom stood for a while, looking them over. He could see that some of them were wondering why he didn't just get on with it, as did Fred and John, who were squirming a bit at the table. They were next to speak.

"Good evening your worship and all you fine people," started Tom, "I don't know any of you and wanted to check you all out before I took any action. You see, when you are in battle facing a whole lot of enemy, you do not pick up your gun and start shooting. First you have to remember how many blokes and guns we've got. Then you check out the enemy and guess at how many he's got. Then you wonder if you start shooting, where will they run to and hide. Then you look around and wonder where you are going to run to and hide. You see, war is not easy.

It's not like your local Rugby game next week-end. You can't put out fake reports about your best blokes being injured. You can't have interviews with the press and complain about how muddy the field is and how your blokes are useless in the mud. Your opposing rugby teams may buy these stories but let me assure you, the Germans do not". The Rugby analogy raised a few chuckles and nodding of heads, with some knowing winks.

"The winner of any battle is usually the team that did the most preparation. The team that practiced the most was, an awful lot of time, the luckiest team. Generally, any battle can be won by any team, on any given day but the war, with all those battles put together, is always won by the team with the best equipment and the healthiest men who are well rested men plus the team that can quickly replenish equipment. An army trying to win a war cannot do so if they cannot get supplies. Clean uniforms, fresh food, warm blankets, medicines and the latest weapons, ammunition, oil and fuel, are essential. And we get a lot from our friends in India, Australia, New Zealand and Canada. If it wasn't for those countries we may be in a position of surrendering soon. However, we are running thin.

I fought alongside South African troops who were very brave and never gave up. I made a very good friend of one, Piet Joubert, who was as brave as anyone I ever knew. In fact he is off now volunteering to fight alongside some French resistance fighters. He wants to show them better ways to ambush Germans. Piet wants to fight alongside the Americans when they arrive in North Africa in a few weeks. At last the USA was in the war. This did not mean the war was over, or even soon to be over, but it did add optimism that the war would now be over quicker, and a damn good chance that the Germans would lose.

As you all know, the USA will be in with our troops. General George Patton will be in North Africa very soon, perhaps two months from now and that alone should help push Rommel out forever. I met Rommel once and shook his hand as he spoke to us. He was not any superman, he simply had an efficient army and he was being constantly replenished by his behind-the-scenes workers. But he would kill you as easy as buttering a piece of toast if you ever stood in his way.

So, when you are sitting around wondering how you can support your own boys as well as a lot of other Mother's boys, concentrate on replenishment for us. It could be easier than you think. Australia is supplying us with woolen bedding, clothing and so on. Why? Well they have lots of sheep. New Zealand sends food, why? Because they have lots of sheep and lots of fruit. South Africa has sheep, and fruit, but also metals and mines. Have you ever volunteered to allow Simonstown, your huge navy base, to be used for repairing damaged ships in battles from this hemisphere? Repairing aircraft by making panels of alluminium to order.

Here is an example: I can tell you that a few cans of South African Pilchards saved a number of Prisoners of War and I was one of them. Where they came from I do not know, but that small amount of food helped keep us alive and able to be and stay alert. Imagine feeding a couple of hundred active allied soldiers with pilchards, beef, cooked chicken, and dairy products, like powdered milk. Some will say they were never asked; others say they volunteered and nobody got back to them. Well, it is pretty chaotic pushing paper in wartime, so volunteer again. Maybe your idea just got lost in the mail. Maybe there was a reply and it fell through the cracks at your end. Just try again.

We do not have the luxury of deciding who we want to live like after the war. Hitler has shown his hand today. Most of the few Hitler worshippers that ever existed have converted to anti-Hitlerism. They have seen what his plans are and they don't like them at all. But getting rid of him will not be easy, so I urge you to support our efforts and please don't let us fade away and then wonder how it was that we all lost. Any questions?"

"Ja man, listen was that Piet Joubert the bloke that used to chase Rhinos here before the war?" asked a dapper man dressed like a banker, in the front row?'

"Yes Sir, that is exactly who he is" replied Tom.

"Well, if that's the case I am going to ask Britain for some blue-prints and my steel factory from here on will make whatever metal parts they want for the war effort. If all the troops are like him, we cannot let them fight without massive support from us." The entire audience rose and applauded. In thirty minutes, just being himself, Tom had secured a very generous donation.

Then Tom said, "I must sit down now and have a nice cold Castle beer. I thank you all for listening." As Tom sat there was a quick huddle around the other two men, John and Fred, and it was agreed that they would not speak at all tonight, as Tom had done the job. They would speak at the next venue, two days later at the commonwealth club, where the audience might be almost entirely professional sportsmen, current and retired. Fred and John both sighed with relief and the trio ordered beers.

This routine went on three times in Cape Town, and each man gave great speeches and won over the hearts of many. The three men were put on a DC4, the Norwegian Air force troop carrying aircraft, and flown to Johannesburg one afternoon. They did a speech each at the General Hotel and were flown back at midnight, to Cape Town. Not quite the heartwarming audience they found in Cape Town but still more positive than negative. Some business people agreed to begin using their factories to supply food and clothing, as well as boots and shoes. So, the idea worked and soon the trio would sail back to Southampton.

The three men were treated to a "Braaivleis" (a BBQ) on a farm just outside Paarl, a lovely little town just outside Cape Town, known for its wine and fruit. They learned how the South Africans celebrated. Lots of meat and corn on the cob simply grilled naked on the searing hot fire (A Braai) over local wood, next to the rump steaks and lamb chops, boerewors, (a traditional farmer's sausage) and of course, lots of great wine and terrific beer. Tom especially liked the KWV Cabernet Sauvignon and found a case of it at a duty free store at the dockside. He took it to England and those twelve bottles lasted him nearly a year.

Then it was all over. The trio boarded the Arundel Castle and left Cape Town on January 5th 1942. The Arundel Castle stopped in Madeira, for a day, on a blustery January. The trio did not bother touring the island but managed to take a taxi to a local bar. Lovely wine caused them to keep sampling it, which caused them to become knee-walking, and later commode-hugging, drunk. They had no dinner on board when they returned to the ship, and retired to their bunks and slept until 1100. Tea and plain toast was all they could get down them and they napped until 1900. Then they went down to dinner and ate heartily, mostly a beef stew and lots of mashed potato.

At 0500 on January 21st 1942, the Arundel slipped into the docks at Southampton and tied up. Tom found a telegram slid under his Cabin door and it read: "Welcome home. Good work we hear. Report to ships desk for envelope with instructions for all three. See you later today." The envelope at the desk contained Five Pounds and an address. The enclosed note said "buy yourselves lunch, NO BOOZE. Use balance for Taxi to 422 Shirley Road, in the corner bar, at 1500. Regs. Dowdall".

The trio disembarked, into the grey, grizzly, winter weather; so bleak after Africa and beautiful seas. They headed for a taxi rank and asked the driver to take them to the address shown. It was 1000 and they guessed that it would be easier to pay for the taxi first, then grab a bite to eat once at their destination, then simply walk over at 1500.

After egg and chips at a nearby café, they walked over to meet Dowdall. He was very busy and said, "look here, chaps, here are envelopes for each of you. I wanted to see you again and thank you for a job well done. I am afraid the war carries on, and we are all still in it. Each of us has a job to do, so Pawson and Atkins, you are free to go. Follow instructions in your envelopes, and may you both have God-Speed. Gale, I need you to stay behind with me.

Goodbye chaps; really nice to know you. Let's all plan on meeting right here in this pub, after the war. You can call Captain Clarkson's office and he will put us all together. Invite him too." They all shook hands and John and Fred saluted Dowdall, then hugged Tom, and left.

"Right" said Dowdall, "I need an assistant and one that can make decisions as well as stand in for me when I am not around. I am asking you, Tom, to make a decision today. A little boring is what you might think but far from it. You will be mostly in England and I can't see how it would ever be possible for you ever to be captured by the Germans ever again. Well, alright, captured, possibly, but for sure never sunk in one of their blasted ships."

"Well, as long as I am not in a position where my mates think I have a cushy job and am shirking my duty fighting on the front line against gerry, I would appreciate the position," replied Tom.

"Believe me, Gale," said Dowdall, "the best armies win wars because they also have back-room boys who can make sure the front-line gets supplies and everything they need. Without us the front line is helpless. We feed off each other and your job will be the most important contribution to the war effort than any other job you've had. Maybe not quite as dangerous, but then 90% of our front-line troops will never have been in the type of danger you were caught up in. So, just say yes, and thank me at the end of the war, for the most satisfying job you've had, in the army."

"Okay, you're on Sir," beamed Tom.

Sadly, Tom learned that many or most of the casualties of war filtered through his office. It was not just deaths being reported but "incidents" that could be printed so the public and the armed forces could read about exploits that could boost their morale, perhaps, or simply report a story that would make the forces be more alert as the dangers increased. Dowdall was truly a propaganda man.

By August 1942, Field Marshall Bernard Montgomery had been appointed in North Africa. Tom got to hear about the exploits to oust Rommel who was still there, still creating havoc, and apparently, still beating the hell out of the Allies. On the one hand, Tom wished he could have been in those battles, and be on the winning side for once. But he was very content to simply do his job where he was. Tom was also not alongside the American, 4 star General Patton, who arrived with a lot of bluster and truly helped enormously with morale. The British had experience but had been pounded so often by Rommel that they were becoming defeatist in attitude, and apparently the never-ending leadership issues never solved much. The Americans were bright and fresh and equipped and eager to fight, but had never experienced battle. So, on paper at least, Rommel's chances looked pretty optimistic. Once again, those best laid plans can come back and bite you hard.

The Americans learned quickly in one dreadful battle against Rommel, in Kasserine Pass, starting in December 1942. With every advantage on their side, Rommel trounced them. But this would be his last victory. The Americans discovered what not to do, and Patton whipped them into a fine fighting force. And, with lots of rivalry in the mix, the British troops picked themselves up and became the powerful fighting force they always were. For a while there they had absented themselves on a mental holiday. It was pure ego between Montgomery and Patton and Rommel. Too bad Tom missed it. No more adventures for him. As Rommel said "for you ze war is over!" As far as fighting it seemed over for Tom, but it still was war and Tom felt it every day for two-and-a-half more years.

A very sad day for Tom was in July 1943, when he learned of the death of Piet Joubert. He was with Montgomery's army in Sicily, and was driving a Jeep when a sheep farmer in front of him herded his flock into a booby-trapped device over a bridge. The Germans were retreating and often left traps behind. About a hundred sheep, their shepherd and Piet and his vehicle, tumbled through a gaping hole in the bridge, onto rocks some hundred feet below. Piet deserved a hero's death, more along the lines of him alone, say, taking out an enemy machine gun unit, with him killing a thousand men before he ran out of ammunition and, even then, ran at the few enemy alive and bayoneted them before he was shot and killed himself. Tom was really saddened because Piet had died, but also by the insignificant manner in which he died.

Tom became extremely satisfied at his job. He toiled at first, learning how to put together battle reports, then help strategize how best to use information to help future battles. Every day Tom agonized over not being in the front line, somewhere, yet realizing how helpful his limited but useful knowledge was assisting the war effort.

"You've got to look at the big picture, Tom" lectured Dowdall, almost monthly.

Toward the middle of January, 1945 Tom was advised that both Fred and John had both died in a battle in the Ardenne while their 1st Northamptonshire unit had been cut off by German Panzers. They and a handful of other British soldiers, joined up with some stragglers cut off from their American 84th Unit. Both allies had been re-capturing the town of La Roche en-Ardenne. A number of posthumous medals had been awarded to this joint Allied unit that, with few vehicles, but armed to the teeth, destroyed over twenty Panzers, mostly with captured German rocket propelled grenade's, and killed over two hundred German troops. Sadly, with only a total of forty-five allied troops, they were outnumbered eventually and all slaughtered, and some still say, by firing squad. The Germans were becoming frightened and no prisoners were being taken at that stage of the war. There was rumoured to be a notorious SS Panzer group who were responsible for some direct firing squad slaughters of Allied troops and this appeared to be the case here.

Tom was truly saddened at this news, as he knew that there by the grace of God, his final hours on earth would likely have been with those two men and his fate would have been the same. Still, it was pure conjecture, and he had a job to do. No time for moping. And so, Tom ended the war in the busiest, most satisfying and fun job he'd ever had. "At one time, for about two years, I was like the proverbial fly on the wall. I got to hear about every battle and every incident, along with precise details as to losses and gains, as if I had been there taking it all in." Tom ended up supervising the building of army barracks, army headquarters and military defensive installations all along the south coast, especially around the White Cliffs of Dover. He said "I had an army uniform but I was mostly behind my desk or riding in a Jeep or out there being a building foreman."

There never was a re-union in that pub in Plymouth. Col. Dowdall emigrated to New Zealand and Captain Clarkson died of some form of cancer, at a very early age in 1949. Tom went into business for himself, using many skills he had learned in the army and he took up residence in Sussex.

19

A NEW DIRECTION FOR BETTE

Bette was asked if she could wind up her job as an ambulance driver in May, 1945. She had been taught to drive before the war but now had the British Army instructing her. How to think which gear she was in, and why. How to change old driving habits when it was raining, by using gears to slow down and not rely solely on the brakes. She loved the camaraderie of all the other drivers, most of them women, and the days when she was off she simply enjoyed being with other off-duty drivers and go the cinema or for a meal somewhere. She said it taught her much improved social skills and interaction with strangers. She had not lived a sheltered life but she had selected who she wanted to mix with. Now she had no choice but to mix with people from all walks of life, and she liked it.

The war was not over yet but the bombing of England had stopped long ago and some sort of normality was approaching at most hospitals. The ambulances were now needed as simple transportation of goods and food from the docks to the general populace, who were slowly emerging from the very strict rationing to a slightly more relaxed ration system. Still no white flour or luxury foods, but vegetables were available as required, and more meat was on the menu than before. Just getting them from English farms to Grocers was the urgent need and re-vamped ambulances would help a lot. Britain's experiment during the war to ask the populace to set up gardens and grow vegetables was a tremendous success. Now, as the war slowly wound down, many of those same amateur gardeners had taken up expanded gardens and the work had become full-time. They really helped the average person by providing good wholesome vegetables. Many went on to become wealthy farmers and exist to this day as huge suppliers of fresh foods.

It was about a week of doing nothing, sharing a flat with her good friend, Gracie, near Marble Arch, that Bette started to feel "edgy". "I need money and something to do," she told Gracie, so she went out job hunting. The first day she took some clothing in to a local laundry and cleaners. She waited a long while at the counter for service, and finally a very smartly dressed elderly man approached her and said, "Could you help me back here. I am on my own and my workers are on lunch and you are a bit taller than me. I cannot reach the switch at the top of my dryer and its running too hot. Turn it down for me and I will do your order free."

Bette thought that was a fair deal and went around the counter, to the back office. She stood on her toes and flicked the switch. "There you are," she said, "you need to change the position of any switches that you need to get at frequently. What you need, my man, is a decent electrician to come in here and do it quickly. Get your manager to call one immediately."

"That's the problem," he replied, "I just re-started this business a few months ago now the war seems close to ending and I don't have a manager and I am too busy doing the books. You don't know a good reliable book-keeper do you?"

Bette said, "Well, I am a qualified bookkeeper. I used to do the books at Jacobs Cleaners, not far from here, before the war. Now I suppose I could be available, but I would need a good pay if I was also being the manager. How much are you willing to pay then?"

"Oh I wasn't hinting at you, Madam," he blushed, "but I would pay four quid a week."

"Make it six quid and I will do both jobs starting right now, if you like." Said Bette.

"I like," replied Horace McMichael, owner of Carlton Cleaners, and a married man with 3 children under age ten. But I would like you to leave your clothing order here and go home and design a job application form on a typewriter. Get twenty copies made and fill in one form with your details and file the rest in your office. And bring along the receipts for your reimbursement.

Your hours will be eight a.m. to three p.m., Monday to Friday, and every other Saturday off, with eight a.m. to six p.m. on the Saturday you work. Closed on Sundays of course. If all that suits you, then see you tomorrow at eight a.m. Ooh! I'm quite excited at this".

"So am I and I believe in fate, I think we will make a good team. Mind you unless you fire me, I shall be looking for regular pay increases as we go along," beamed Bette as she left the cleaners premises. The tinkle of the little bell on the entrance door stayed in her head all the way home, which, by the way, was just around the corner, maybe 500 yards. How convenient.

The next day at seven forty five a.m. Bette waited outside the door in a light drizzle and a minute later Horace arrived. " Good morning Mr. Mc Michael, obviously I need a key. Standing in the rain does not thrill me too much," said Bette.

Horace responded apologetically, "please call me Horace and take my key. Three doors down is a shop that will make a duplicate for you. Maybe around your lunch break you could get it done, and thanks for helping out".

Bette worked happily for almost seven years, with no events occurring to "keep my adrenalin popping" at this establishment until 1952. Bette visited friends and ate out three or four times a week, with mostly her friend Gracie. They both loved the cinema and now and then would visit a race track where they usually broke even, placing bets on the horses. Of course there was the occasional "date" with some gentleman one or the other had just met. The two women shared every moment discussing every moment when it came to dating. No man passed any test and they simply had fun. Life just seemed so pleasant after the terrible conditions during the war; they, as most people did, just relaxed and enjoyed every single day.

Horace said one day that his wife wanted to take the children and live closer to her family in Clacton, a small seaside town not far from London. Not far but almost impossible to do a daily commute from there and he was going to sell the business, Bette recognized the little gold mine that it was and offered to buy it, at almost his asking price, if she could pay him a small down payment and then the balance monthly for five years. The entire business would revert to him if she ever defaulted. He agreed and thus Bette became the owner of Carlton Cleaners.

One night, Bette and Gracie were out at a bar, the Three Tuns, near Marble Arch, built in 1688, a very popular place to be seen. Bette didn't care if she was seen, the pub happened to be less than one bus stop from her flat with Gracie, so they usually walked over twice a week. Bette always enjoyed a good steak and kidney pudding there, with chips and mushy peas: "That meal keeps me full for three days, " she explained, "Salads and cucumber sarnies after that, so I actually lose weight".

In the bar the two of them struck up a conversation with a banker, and he explained that his obsession was old classic cars. He belonged to the Vintage Automobile Society and every year they raced from London to Brighton. It was a sixty mile run, first started in 1896, and most cars were built before 1905. As it was run on the first Sunday of November, every year, he would be getting ready in about ten days. He asked both women to have dinner with him and his family, in Brighton, on the Monday night following the run. He gave them the name of the hotel where most participants and their guests stayed at and said he would ensure they had a room to share. Well, this was something new for Bette and so she said yes. Bette really loved those old cars while Gracie never did seem to fit in. They stayed friends and shared the same flat for many years, but Bette now had a new crowd to hang around with. It was mutual, the car owners liked her too and every year Bette participated in the rally.

1952 was a busy year and as Autumn set in, Bette met an American business-man at a party of Veteran Car owners. He was alone in England. His family was all back in USA and he owned a 1905 De Dion Bouton car. He asked Bette if she could be his passenger on the London to Brighton veteran car run, the next month. She liked this man, and if the rules said a passenger was required, then she would gladly oblige.

They became very good friends, and possibly more, but that part of Bette's life was very private. No doubt they were close as two events occurred that dramatically changed Bette's life. One night, over dinner at the Savoy Grill, David Grey, her wealthy American friend, told Bette, "One of my friends has a son whom he wanted to run a business. Would you ever consider selling your cleaning business? And, if you did, would you then con-sider working with me in my factory, in Slough, near Heathrow Airport. You know my business manufactures zinc toothpaste tubes, which I then supply to various UK and European toothpaste factories, by the millions. You would earn far more than you are taking out now and you would be given shares in the business. But also, you would have a say in making any efficiency improvements, and we could be close together, etc. Say yes." Bette liked the "etc."

She sold the cleaners for twice more than she paid for it. She paid off Horace in a lump sum and started work for David at twice her previous take-home pay plus 20% ownership in the factory. Bette loved everything about her new job as General Manager. She spent most of her days working and on weekends, she got together with the Vintage Car crowd, with David, and spent many days, riding "shotgun" in lovely old cars, French and British, with a few German editions. Bette was well liked and her life was socially and mentally, very gratifying. Bette had a most wonderful social life which lasted almost eighteen years. It was dinners, films, car rallies and enjoying David.

In 1970 it all came to an end. David died of a heart problem and Bette was left to manage a factory and her social life came to an abrupt end. She tried going once or twice to the Veterans Car Club meetings, but with no partner, she felt lost. Her friend Gracie had married and moved to New Zealand, so she really became a hard-working but almost reclusive figure. Her main recreation was her membership in the Oval Cricket Club, where she initially volunteered to help in the accounting department. She had dated a man who was a member and he introduced her to the club.

A week after David's death a registered letter from a law firm in Oxford Street changed everything. The factory had been left entirely to Bette along with the advice from David, in a letter he had hand-written, a few weeks prior to his death, stating:

"Dear Bette, Thank you for making my life so worthwhile. If you are reading this, I am obviously not on this earth any longer and you are now the owner of my factory, and it couldn't be owned by anyone more deserving. You are at complete liberty to do whatever you wish as the new owner, but I have a suggestion that you should act on it promptly, if you agree of course. Plastics are now becoming a new and more practical element to manufacture items, and I believe it will take over the toothpaste tube industry, as an example, one day. It would be far too expensive to try to convert our factory (well, yours now) into a plastic moulding version. I suggest you seek out a potential buyer soon, and get rid of it while you can still demand a good price. I believe you could sell it for a quarter of a million pounds, and if you can, do so. You might have a window of opportunity to sell within three years. This is enough for a prospective buyer to make some return and for you to sell at its peak price. And, by the way, you also own a 1905 De Dion Bouton. Speak to Hartley Anderson, owner of Suffolk's Garage, and he will advise you. I miss you already. We will meet again one day but not too soon, I hope, for your sake!

Love, David. Signed January 22nd 1970"

No mention was ever made of David's family in America. Any communication to them was not known to Bette and neither was she interested in knowing. It was revealed a decade later that the family in the USA was extremely wealthy and had actually not even known what their estranged husband and son-in-law were even up to in England.

Bette, with a heartbreaking start to her life, was now a lady of leisure with a substantial amount of money. What her relationship was with the American is not really known. She steadfastly maintained that it was purely business, always platonic and, except for a kiss on the cheek on New Year's Eve, that was it. We shall never know but nobody believed her. How long she would be able to now stay 'at leisure' would be interesting.

One of her first efforts to getting involved in society again was to see if she could help younger brother, George. Most, of his upper teeth had been smashed out of his mouth, during the war, shattered with nerve endings revealed and in shocking pain. Just recently, however, she heard that George's prosthetics were mediocre and today, many years afterwards, he had begun whistling a bit when he spoke and had an awkward jaw alignment situation.

Bette found a specialist in London, referred by an influential investment Banker from the Vintage Car Club. She asked him to examine George and simply fix him up with the absolute state-of- the-art prosthetics that would be as close to real teeth as possible, and asked him to lie to George that this was a Government issue and that George would not have to pay anything. The big lie was difficult as George had left the Royal Marines and had joined the London Dock Police. However, she convinced the Assistant Commissioner of Police, whom she had met at the Veterans Car Club years ago, to allow George to go to London and take a week off, and with pay.

George had three appointments, with Bette picking him up in her spanky new Hillman Minx car, and driving him each way for forty minutes and waiting at the specialist's office. Poor George, only fifty-five years old, went through hell, but emerged with a perfect set of ceramic-on-metal teeth, fixed to his old sheared-off teeth, and never knew Bette had picked up the tab at some three thousand Pounds.

20

TOM STILL BATTLES ON

Tom was summoned to the Pensions headquarters of the UK Army, in 1946. Ironically the office was less than a block from the army office Tom worked in until the war ended. He was asked to visit with a Major Humphries, who sat across from a row of chairs in an enormous office, and, peering over his glasses at Tom, said, "Now Mr. Gale, you were demobbed last year and you have been sent five letters asking you to come in to see us about your pension. You see, we have checked your whereabouts during the war, and calculated all income due to you based on your capture, twice, and your foreign country participation, plus your rise in rank. You are due thirteen pounds fourteen shillings and seven pence a month pension, starting at age sixty-five. But you need to confirm certain facts and agree to update us each time you move. Why have you ignored us?"

Tom said, "The reason is because I don't want your pension. I believe that money should only go to the dependents of all those blokes what died fighting for this bloody country. I lived, and I don't deserve it and even if I did, I don't want it. I want to forget the war. Where can I sign to order you lot to stop bothering me?"

"Well, cough, cough, splutter and harrumph," muttered the Major, "this is unusual but I suppose if you sign here," shoving an official piece of army letterhead at Tom, "print your name and then print DECLINE and sign underneath, that will stop all further contact. Are you sure about this?"

"Give it 'ere," said Tom, signing and writing. "That's it. I am now leaving, I will not be back." With that Tom left and never did receive any further communication from the army, and, of course, never did receive any pension money either. Precisely what he wanted.

Tom married a lovely lady in 1950 and had two boys, John and Richard. The marriage was absolutely a happy and normal union and for Tom, civilian life was just fine. His Wife was well known in the medical research field and between them all life was okay.

Tom and his family lived a quiet and normal life until the two boys became teenagers. Then a dramatic change happened,

21

BETTE'S LIFE TOPSY TURVY

Bette spent a good deal of her waking hours with her friends and relatives. She always asked George to smile, each time she dropped by his house. He always did and his teeth looked terrific. She doted on all her nephews and nieces and she invested in a very nice flat near Earls Court, on Pennywern Road "far enough away from all the relatives and near enough to the tube station to visit them if I want," she said.

For almost a decade, in the 1950's and through to the early 1960's, Bette was a member of the Cricket Council at the Oval Cricket Grounds. She started as a volunteer, helping in the accounts of the Surrey Cricket Club, and then, because she was Bette, who was a bit bossy but very efficient and skilled, she was asked to sit on the board. Her life really was fun. If she had been a man she would be having a great bachelor's life. There was something missing in her life, however, a partner. It was not that she wanted one or was even thinking of one, but she seemed to glow when she was around her family: George, his wife, Pat and their children. She had lots of friends and relatives, single and married, with children and without and she spent many nights visiting them. Visits to the cinema or shopping with girl-friends, or dinner out, but seldom a serious relationship with any man. She had only loved Jack Simmons and that event seemed so far distant she found it hard to remember his face.

Her best friend since well before the war, was Kitty. Kitty had a brother, Tom Gale. She barely remembered him from some time before the war. Once or twice at a picnic with his family and other friends, but she could not remember if she had ever even shaken his hand. His name arose when his sister phoned Bette one day and said that there was to be a 10th anniversary party at Tom's house soon, and would Bette come. She said she would. She rather liked that invitation and put it in her diary. The party never happened. Bette never knew why; she waited for an invitation and one never came. She wondered to herself why she was so disappointed that a simple house-party invitation hadn't arrived, when she herself was leading such an active and fun-filled social life. Maybe fate might cause a change; it had before.

One day, in late 1970, with Bette now in her fifties and living a routine that she was comfortable with, fate again arrived. She was sitting alone in her flat, watching her newly purchased colour TV, the best she could buy with a huge 13 inch screen. She was nodding off as the show was a bit too dull for her, a re-run film, called, "Carry on Regardless", one of those old British "Carry

On Gang' films, in Black and White. "What's the point in spending good money on a colour TV when half the time the rubbish they show is in black and white?" she would rant. The humour really was harsh and unfunny with lots of smut and just as Bette was reaching over to turn the wretched machine off, the phone rang. Typically she answered " hello, this is 01 43219," never saying her name.

The male voice on the other end of the phone said "Is that Elizabeth Swan?"

"No," she replied, "it's Bette Simmons. What do you want, who are you?"

"Your friend is Kitty Gale," he said, "that's my sister. I'm Tom Gale, we used to know each other a bit, before the war. Do you remember me? Are you married? Why is your name different?"

Bette replied "I am a widow now. Yes of course I know who you are. You got married after the war. How is your wife, and your two boys?"

There was a silence and a big deep breath from the other end of the line, and Tom said, "Well that's the reason I am calling you, I need some help and I kept thinking of you. My wife was killed a year ago in a car accident and I am lost. I have nobody around to help me and I have two boys and they need a Mother and your face keeps appearing when I cry at night. Could we meet and have a chat?"

"Tom I am so sorry for your situation, but how can I help?" "I mean, if we met what could we possibly discuss? I mean, if we talked what would we talk about, I mean well, Yes, I suppose we could at least talk, and maybe

I have some contacts that I know who may be able to help you, but I mean, when, where. I mean it's too late now but perhaps tomorrow?" She was very flustered and didn't know exactly what to say, a complete departure from her usual direct and confident persona.

Tom answered, "Bette thank you, can we meet at your house and I will pick you up. I won't come in just 'onk the 'orn and we can go somewhere where we can have a light snack. Is that okay with you and what time would be best for you, I mean to be outside your door. Of course I would need your address or I wouldn't know where you lived, would I? So if it's okay, give it to me, I have a pencil handy and then I can read it to get to you, you know?"

"Ten, Pennywern Road, Earl's Court. Make it six p.m. and let's decide where to eat when we get going in the car. We may need more than a light snack," Bette said with a bit more composure now.

The next evening you could have set the time by Big Ben. As Tom pulled up outside the address, the gong started to ring six. Bette was at the window with the sheers drawn aside and saw the car pull up. She took a quick glance in the hall mirror, picked up her gloves and beret then wrapped her scarf around her neck and tucked it into her camel-hair pee jacket, and shut the front door.

She tried to maintain full composure as if she were a model gliding down the seven stairs to the pavement. She looked terrific but those high steps didn't quite allow her to look "model-like". She then slid into the passenger seat of a Ford Granada, a nice car, mostly used by factory reps. and salesmen back then. They shook hands and Tom said, "Oh it's so good to be with you Bette. Can we go to the Nelson Tavern? I understand they have a great carvery and their roast beef and yorkshire pud is the best in London. And I don't know about you but I could murder a beer."

Bette replied "That sounds very nice and Shandies are my downfall, so yes. I know the owner of the flats next door to Nelson's and he allows me to park there when I go shopping. I will just put my card on the dashboard so he will know it's me, then we can go in the back door and save us getting wet if it starts to rain."

Their meeting went well and it was obvious that Tom, being the straight-talking, no nonsense gentleman he was, wanted Bette to become his wife and to become a mother to his two boys. But there were moments when the two of them sat there, saying nothing, and peering into the fire.

"I think I shall go up and get a second helping of that beef," suggested Tom, "I can't remember when I had such quality. Anything I can get for you, dear?"

"Get me another Shandy would you please, Tom," asked Bette, as she sat there with her mind racing. This was a rare event for Bette. She had been on a few dates with other men, of course, but not many. This one had her trembling inside. It just felt different.

She did have a good life, although without anyone to share it with, but was that even important to her? She asked herself. She had enough money to travel and she had gone many times to Europe. Then Australia to visit a niece. Canada to visit a nephew (me) and various parts of the USA. She owned her own flat, mortgage-free and a nice car. But something was telling her not to lose out on what appeared to be an opportunity to perhaps make her life whole. Maybe Tom was worth pursuing? Then she almost rapped her own knuckles. Stop thinking ahead, let this roll along at its own pace, and see what develops. Maybe nothing will, what if I don't like him very much, who knows?

"Well," Bette asked, "how are you managing to make a living and look after two children now, Tom?" She had called Kitty, Tom's sister, that morning, to find out what was going on. So she knew some details. Tom, having refused any pension from the Government, and not being the greatest 'detail' man in the world, was having a rough time, emotionally.

Tom said, "It's not easy, but manageable for a while. They are teenagers, no longer little children but still can't look after themselves, and they are too young to drive. Eventually they will learn to cook and all the household chores that one has to do, but right now they need a bit of hand-holding.

My ex Mother-in-Law comes to the house at 0800, sorry I use military time 'cos I'm used to it. Anyway, she makes sure the two boys get breakfast and makes them a snack for lunch then I drive the three of them to school, drop the boys off and then take her home and drop her off. We always got on but she can't do this much longer with all her ailments. Then she drives to the school to pick them up at 1500, and sometimes stays with them 'til I get home about 1700. She usually has a hot dinner made for us and then she drives to her home. Her husband needs looking after as he was injured in the war and can't walk very well. I tell you, Bette, its all go, aint it?"

Bette said "I would like to visit your house and say hello to your boys. I believe I met them when they were very young at some outing one day a long while ago, I think. Kitty invited me to a picnic all of you were enjoying on the beach. They must be quite grown up now."

"Oh that would be terrific. Yes they are, but still kids, you know. Why don't we meet at my house and we could order in fish and chips? There's a chippy just round the corner from us and the two boys often pick up a meal there. Then you could see our situation as it is after their mum died, and so on."

"Now then, how would we arrange that?" Bette enquired.

"How about you taking the train to Worthing. I will meet you at the station, say the 1650 arrival, and you can see a bit of our town. Then perhaps we can go to my place about 1800. The boys will be on their own and we can spend a quiet evening where we all get to know each other. I can drive you to the station for the 2145 train, if that's not too late?"

"Oh nonsense," retorted Bette, "I am not dragging you out at that time of night, especially after you've had a few drinks. No, I shall call a taxi and catch that train on my own, thank you very much."

"Okay, Bette, anything you say," said Tom. "How about another Shandy and then I shall take you home?"

"Actually, how about a port and lemon?" asked Bette. They discussed the times and the arrangement for the next day, and then agreed to call it a night. Tom dropped her off at her apartment about 2200. With a warm hand-shake, she got out of the car and Tom let her run up the stairs, unlock her door and then with a quick wave, he drove off. Tom then had a nearly ninety minute drive to his home.

Bette could not get to sleep. She was suspicious of the circumstances she found herself in. She did not know what to make of Tom. What if he had heard about her selling the factory? How could anyone know that? Did he know she was quite a wealthy woman? What business was he in anyway and was he possibly after her money? She would get to the bottom of all these doubts the next day, but he had better not think he could pull the wool over her eyes. Hah! Eventually, with the TV blaring its night light and confirming there was nothing more to be seen on that shiny black box that night, Bette turned it off and nodded off at about one a.m., well past her usual eleven p.m. bed-time.

Bette made up her mind the next day. She got up at nine a.m., had a nice bath and then tea and toast, spread with Marmite. Then she got dressed up for her day in Worthing. She put on a Donegal tweed suit and comfort-able walking shoes and left her flat for Victoria Station at two p.m. The train for Worthing left Victoria station at two forty five p.m.. She sat in a first class coach, with the Daily Mail newspaper and a tourist's guide to Worthing, which she had purchased at the platform stationers.

The journey went through some of England's most spectacular countryside. For some reason Bette believed the sun shone brighter in Sussex. The rolling hills and the different colour of each field. Newly plowed bright earth, then pale green shoots from new plants and bright, darker green trees bearing apples and pears. Labourers filling sacks with strawberries in other fields. The trip was simply a lovely experience. The train stopped at Worthing at four twenty seven p.m. or 1627 if you were Tom. He was there waiting on the platform. He took Bette's case and her elbow and led her outside to his car, which, she noticed, had been cleaned and polished to showroom condition.

Once she was comfortable in the car, Tom started his Tour of Worthing extravaganza, as if he felt this was his duty to do so. "Now then we have just seen the main station and over here is the ancient bridge that goes over a small inlet from the sea. As we wind our way down Chapel Road we aim for Marine Parade, which runs along the seaside. We could stop anywhere if you want Bette, it's a lovely little town. I think you would like it once you got to know it."

"Tom, can I ask you a question?" she blurted out. "Do you want me to marry you and me live down here with you? What would we do for money?" Typical Bette; she had the patience of a struck match.

She had sworn to herself that she would see what Tom wanted; after all he made the first move. She wanted to take it easy and had sworn to let Tom guide her, not force decisions herself. Now she had gone and done it, forced their relationship, little as it was at this stage, and just possibly embarrassed Tom. Tom said nothing. He stopped the car and then made an illegal U-turn back up the hill, towards the A27 road to Arundel Castle.

Oh no, Bette thought, he's going back in the direction of the station, maybe he's going to just drop me off and find a less bossy woman? Then, after getting off the main road and turning onto Durrington Hill, he said, "See all these new homes on each side of the road? Well, I built them all, and that one, on the corner over there, is the show home, and I thought we could probably select that one to live in. I am the owner of a house building company, so money is really not a major issue for me, is it for you?"

Bette blanched a little. What she had been so sure of was now off her list. But she did know, from her conversation with Tom's sister, Kitty, that even though he was a good house builder, he had sunk a lot of money into them and the margins for profit were quite thin. So while he was far from poor, he was perhaps not as well off as he was intimating.

Regaining composure she blurted out, "Do you have any idea when this is all supposed to happen?"

Tom said, "Look, I don't know do I. If you see no issues, and you like the idea, why wait? I know it looks like I am being selfish and simply want a mother for my kids over a wife, but it is you that I want." I came looking for you as I always remembered you from before I got married. I didn't go looking for another woman."

Bette remembered later that Tom was at his most romantic at that point. "He never was Tyrone Power, but he was a good man who needed looking after and he found it difficult to express his feelings." Bette was not that much different really, she found it hard to express romantic feelings as well.

He may have been a straight shooter and a 'tell it like it is' man, but he was finding it quite difficult to get through the beginnings of this courtship. Then it became six p.m. and Tom said "time to get home." And he headed for the neighborhood where he lived.

The two boys were waiting by the window when Tom drove into the driveway. "Come in and say hello to the boys. You actually met them once or twice if I had them with me when shopping and you might have been down here with Kitty." he beamed. The two lads, the eldest Richard, seventeen and John fifteen, politely shook hands with Bette and they all retired to the lounge for a cup of tea and biscuits. The boys were excited as they had decided to run down the street and pick up fish and chips and had the money ready. Bette ordered halibut, Tom ordered hake. Both Richard and John had cod and chips; one had mushy peas.

They were back before the tea was made and Bette went into the kitchen and took command and control. Bang, crash, plates were out and the meal was served, the teapot filled and then, within a few minutes, all brought into the dining room. The table already had everyone's favourite condiments: malt vinegar for Tom; brown sauce for Bette; ketchup for both boys and salt, pepper and Wallys , which are enormous dill pickles, for those who wanted them. Everything was consumed with such enthusiasm one would have thought food was about to be banned from the planet.

Afterwards they all went into the lounge and finished their tea. All and sundry were chatting away as if they had all been together for years. It was very obvious that

Bette was a hit with the boys and she was very impressed with their manners and their schooling as well as their demeanor.

"Oh my goodness, "exclaimed Bette, "I've just seen the time, its nine twenty p.m. and that train leaves at ten, ten p.m. so Tom, call me a taxi would you please."

Tom said "You'll be getting to bed late tonight, what time do you usually turn in?"

Bette replied that "Eleven thirty ish, after the news, is my normal bedtime, but nobody has a stopwatch on me, so it could be ten or midnight. Tonight won't upset any great routine for me."

"No, Bette, I can't let you out on your own, I know I agreed last night but tonight I insist that I take you to the station and that will leave the boys, on their own, to do the dishes and put away things that should be put away, isn't that right lads?" puffed Tom.

Bette agreed, she was too tired to argue. "Goodnight Richard and John," and gave each a hug. I've had a very pleasant evening and maybe we shall meet up with you soon." Both kissed her lightly on the cheek.

Then she and Tom drove off, and got to the station at ten p.m., in time for her train. "Thanks for a lovely evening, said Bette. Maybe we could do the same again, but let's go out to a restaurant, or a hotel in Durrington, somewhere, and I can stay over at the hotel. Maybe I could come earlier, say eleven a.m? You could finish the tour you started earlier. I'd like to see Arundel Castle. Could we?"

"Anything you want, Bette."

Bette grabbed the car door handle but then slid over and kissed Tom on the cheek, before getting out of the car and walking fast to the platform where her train had just arrived. Tom acted like a teenage boy who had just been handed the phone number of some girl he had a crush on. "Yes!" he said, hammering his fist on the dashboard. For some reason he whistled 'Zippidee Doodah, Zippidee Yeah," all the way back home.

Bette went to the bank the next day and checked her balance and spoke to an investment adviser about investing in some funds where she could draw a level amount out each month, an annuity, while leaving a separate account with a lump sum in it; "Mad money," she called it, "just in case something comes up and we need temporary financial help."

22

COURTING

Tom did not phone at all that day. It was as if he had been to see a psychiatrist who had advised him to make Bette wait. Don't rush it. Let her make the next move. He hadn't, but it was a sale day and four of his houses had sold, and he had to be at each one, with the lawyer and realtors, so too much to think of and Bette was not in his thoughts at all.

As he parked outside his house that evening, it was nearly 1900 hours, Tom realized how exhausted he was. Building houses had so many issues and so many things that could go wrong. But selling houses was far more intense and while all had sold today, and the finances were all clean, he needed a beer and to put his feet up He also was longing for a conversation with an adult. While Tom's two boys were no longer babies and a decent conversation with either of them was enjoyable and mature, that was not what he was looking for.

He opened a second beer, a Double Diamond, quite light and very refreshing. He drank from the bottle and his shoes had already been kicked off. The two boys had left a note on the fridge door saying they were at the local youth club where there was a Cliff Richard night and lots of new girls. Cliff was England's Elvis, in a way, and the new girls could well be the graduating class from the local convent school, where for sure the girls would be rock and rolling all their convent learning right out the door. At least every teenage boy there would be hoping so.

Tom went into the Kitchen and found no hot meal in the oven so he made a sandwich, as he realized his last meal that day was toast and Marmite for breakfast. There was a Fray Bentos tin of corned beef and a small tin of Heinz baked beans. He went for the beef. He pulled out the white sliced loaf, smeared two slices with butter then opened the corned beef and put about half the tin onto one slice. Found the Colman's hot mustard in a jar and spread a big smear of that on top. Drew out four large brown pickled onions from their jar, and plonked it all together on a plate.

Then he slouched back in his comfy chair, turned on the TV and watched "Gunsmoke." He rather thought of himself as Pa Cartwright and Hoss and Little Joe as his sons and ranch hands. Tom managed to eat most of his sandwich, with only about a quarter of it falling on his shirt and the floor. He finished the second beer and with Cartwright off to fight for land stolen by a ruthless cattle rustling hombre, he fell fast asleep. He awoke still in his chair and still holding a paper napkin to his mouth, as the boys got home around 2330. He was angry at himself as he was going to phone Bette at about 2130. Ah! Well, tomorrow is another day.

Bette realized that she was feeling very blue about not having a call from Tom. She was walking around her flat, watering the ferns, just having had a small lunch even though she was not hungry. In fact, she had lost her appetite lately. She had to eat so forced down a small quiche she had bought at Harrods a few days past, along with a large cup of tea and two biscuits. Now she was at a loss as to what to do.

The fridge was bare and her pantry had very little food and she did need to go shopping, but what if Tom phoned? She would never know if he had and she would kick herself if he had and she missed it. But there again, she figured, I can't stay in every day just because he might phone. Well, she said to herself, to hell with him, I am going out and I don't care if he never phones me again. At that very moment the phone rang; Bette leaped over the watering can and grabbed the phone off the wall by the front door hallway and said calmly, "Oh hello Tom".

"Is that Mrs. Simmons?" asked a lady at the other end. "Post Office here and we have a special delivery for you. Will you be home at four o'clock today for a signature?"

"Oh, well, yes, I mean well, okay, I shall be here at four o'clock."

Now Bette was really disappointed but also now curious as to what the package may be. At four o'clock sharp, she found out. Some months back Bette had enquired at a real estate office on the high street, about a small cottage in the countryside, near Littlehampton, but she needed to know what her London flat would sell for first. She had paid almost twenty eight thousand pounds for her flat. What she had now was an offer from a member of the Vintage Car Society, who needed a flat in Earls Court, as that would be near his business on Cromwell Road. He owned a Rover Car dealership and was making a lot of money. One assumed that in those circles, speaking of money, or showing off one's wealth, was considered quite crass. Still, he was loaded.

He did not want to dicker over the price, he said in his short, hand-written note. He had approached, Solomon Bros., realtors and, ironically, the same one Bette had spoken to eight months ago, who had never responded. Solomon told him that you might want to sell one day, and to approach you directly, leaving him out so Bette would not have to pay commission. They sure like Bette at that club! Would she accept forty five thousand pounds for her flat, cash, as soon as she wished?

Stunned, Bette could not believe the dilemma she was in. Everything could be perfect timing and yet it could all blow up in her face. First things first. She grabbed her phone book to check Tom's number and as she reached the hallway, the phone rang, it was Tom.

"Hello Bette, I have a proposition. Why don't you sell your flat and come and live with us. I could put an extension on the house so you would really have your own private space. You put all your money into your private account as I don't want any of it. Then, when all my unsold houses have sold, there's six left, we all move into that show-home, on the corner, that I pointed out the other night?"

"Oh hello Tom, do you mind if I absorb all that for a while? Your timing is good, can you check something for me please. Can you get on to the blokes in the know and ask them what value they would put on my flat. Remember it, Number 10 Pennywern Road, Earls Court. And, because I haven't got any patience left could you do it now and phone me back, right away. By the way do not call Solomon Brothers....don't ask. You can tell whoever it is to phone me if they have any questions. Okay. Thanks Tom, now go, we can talk later" It was five twenty p.m. when her phone rang. Bette rushed to the phone, and answered; it was Tom.

"Bette I called on my mate Peter Spartlette, who has been helping me buy land and develop property since I started the business before I got married. He's a regular guy and very trustworthy. He knows someone in London and they say you could maybe get forty-three and up thousand quid for your place today. He says you should ask forty-five and settle for no less than forty-three thousand. Don't forget there's 5% commission comes off that number. Now then what's all this about?"

"Tom, I believe fate has knocked on my door again. How about this? I come down tomorrow, Friday, and spend the weekend at a hotel there and come home on Monday night. Then you can show me around Worthing and we can slow down the pace and talk a lot, as we have a lot to talk about"

"Bette that would be wonderful but why spend money at a hotel, when we can find a room for you at the house?"

"Yes, I thought you would say that, but I need to get away every now and then to digest what's been said and how I translate that and what action is better over another. I understand that you have the best of intentions and I do appreciate the offer, but the hotel would be perfect for me and actually, both of us, if you see what I mean?"

"Okay my dear," said Tom, "I will make a reservation for you in the Burlington hotel which opened in 1865 and is right on the seaside, near the pier. So if you want to spend some time contemplating, this is about the best place to contemplate. They also serve great grub and we can have a meal there one night. Is that alright then?"

"Perfect, I shall rely on your judgment" said Bette, "is it alright for me to catch the nine-thirty and arrive at eleven-ten a.m.?" she asked.

""I shall be there with flowers, smiling as you step off the train."

"Well I don't want flowers and you shouldn't be giving them to me until I have given you something first, but meeting me at the station is terrific. And then take me to the hotel right away so I can get out of my train clothes and into my 'Touring Worthing outfit'. And no fancy ideas now, you'll be downstairs getting us a table for dinner tonight. You rascal, I know what you men are like."

"We shall see you at the station at 1100, Bye love."

Bette was truly excited. Everything was going her way and she really had the world in her hands and she could design her future the way she wanted. She actually hung up the phone realizing that she liked Tom a great deal and it was very obvious that he liked her.

23

A GUIDING LIGHT

Tom was there grinning like a Cheshire cat. The train was a few minutes early but Tom was on the platform when Bette alighted, with a large suitcase. He's keen, thought Bette, been here a while even though the train is early. Bloody hell, thought Tom, she looks like she's planning a round the world cruise, with that suitcase. Hmm! maybe it's just not full.

Bette walked over and gave Tom a big hug and a peck on the cheek. This was the first time she had shown such fondness and Tom could feel her relaxed manner. She was not as suspicious and tense as on previous get-togethers. What a fine woman she was, mused Tom, I must make sure I do this the right way. He opened the car door, and Bette slid in and they drove off to the hotel Burlington.

The lift was right next to the front desk and, unlike many hotel lifts in the south of England, this lift had enough room to hold both of them and the large suitcase.

They got out on the fifth floor and Tom carried the suit-case to room 502, which had a lovely view of the pier, to the left and the ocean all at the front. Bette opened the window and the fresh air streamed in. She took off her heavy suit coat and her hat, then excused herself. "Give me about half an hour, Tom, you could get us a dinner reservation and have a beer in the lounge. I'll make my own way down and then we can head off on the tour. Okay dear?" She kissed him hard on the lips then turned and went into the bathroom.

Tom did as he was told and went down to the lounge, ordered a table for two for 1900, and then sat in a comfy chair with the local newspaper and a draft of a new beer from Australia, called Fosters. It was ice cold and went down very well. "I think I found a new beer," said Tom, nodding at the barman.

The Hotel was nearly 100 years old and it had deteriorated from the end of WW I and was almost demolished in 1960. Fortunately a forward-thinking new owner purchased the property in 1962. He recognized the glorious architecture of pillars and dormers, with lots of light entering the many small brass fitted windows. This had been the original owner's dream hotel a hundred years ago and the new owner wanted to regain the former splendor. As a result of his vision, the hotel was now extremely cosy and the wallpaper with pale lilac roses along with white trim doors and ceilings, added to the allure.

Bette arrived looking fresh in a turquoise summery outfit and a large hat in her hands. They agreed to get going right away and have lunch somewhere on the Worthing tour, within an hour, as both were quite peckish. They drove around and eventually went to Arundel Castle. This castle was built in 1067 during the reign of William the Conquerer. It was damaged in the English Civil War. Fully restored in the 18th and 19th centuries, it is a magnificent building in a very romantic setting. Tom and Bette spent two hours just walking around the lovely grounds. Finding a bench in the shade of a huge 600 year-old oak tree, they sat down and took their breath and talked.

"Tom, I will say this, I see your boys need a mother and you need some hand-holding yourself. I think we could live together without throwing pots and pans at each other, well not every day anyway."

"Bette I don't know why we didn't get married in the first place. How did it all go wrong?" You fancied a sailor and I met a lady at a dance one evening and we just slipped out of each other's lives. You hardly noticed me when we were all kids before the war, but its now today and we can't go back and we can't reverse what's 'appened and now we are 'ere, trying to make a very big decision. I have made mine, I want you to be my wife. I want you to move into the house. I want you to add a woman's touch to it and help the boys grow up right. And I cannot wait. Let's do it now."

A little tear ran down Bette's cheek as she trembled a bit and took Tom's hand. "I don't know how I feel about you and me, you know, out here in the park it's quite easy. But eventually we will have to share a room and then a bed, and I am not sure how I will react to manly advances. It has been a very long time since I have been with a man. I hope you know what I mean when I say that. I mean undressed and feeling him and his intentions. What if I couldn't do that part of being a wife?"

"Why don't you kiss me right now?" said Tom, and he leaned into Bette and gently kissed her on the mouth. She responded until she realized where she was.

"Tom, stop, there are people walking by and watching us. Maybe later when we are alone?"

They got back into the car and spent a few hours driving around Worthing. Tom was not as talkative as he was days before. Bette wanted to see the show home Tom had built, so he drove there. They parked on the road, right outside the house. Bette asked "Is there was anything special about it, compared to all the others you built?"

"Well, it has the best flooring and the best Kitchen cabinets and appliances. The finish on all the wood, and it is not plywood, like the banisters on the stairs, is superior and, the house happens to be one brick row higher than any house in the area, mine and others," explained Tom. "It also has a back entrance directly into the kitchen, with a shed built in right outside, as well as French doors, with triple-paned glass, leading to the back garden from the Dining Room and Lounge area. Upstairs there are three bedrooms and two full bathrooms. There is a toilet just off the kitchen in the hallway," Tom said with pride.

"Is it vacant now? Do you have keys for it?" asked Bette.

"Of course. Want to look it over?" replied Tom.

Bette was very pleasantly surprised when she entered the house. It was fully furnished, but beyond any type of style she could have imagined. Very stylish; perfectly suited for the house and obviously with a designer involved. They went up the stairs and checked out the bedrooms.

"Is that a Queen-sized mattress?" asked Bette.

"I have no idea" said Tom, "I believe it is, I just know it's very comfy. I tested it one night and fell asleep. Here you try it." He helped her sit on the edge of the bed and she swung her legs up and lay on one side.

Patting the side next to her she said, "Well come and lie next to me. See if we fit." So he did. They lay together almost rigid as neither knew what would happen next, or even what they wanted to happen next. Their hands were so close and their bodies parallel to each other from shoulder to knees maybe an inch apart. Both looking straight up at the ceiling.

Bette said after ten minutes or so, "Well you're not one of them men that takes advantage of a helpless woman, are you?"

Tom, almost stuttering replied "Well it's not as if I haven't been thinking of it, but I just remembered what you said earlier on about you being afraid of a man making advances."

"But there are no people walking by now, so now might be a good opportunity to kiss me again. Come here you" she said, grabbing Tom and kissing him hard. He responded very vigorously and, even though it is assumed nothing really happened beyond that kiss, Bette never ever told anyone; certainly not me.

Later on, back at the hotel room, where Tom was not invited in, Bette had a long warm shower and went to bed early. They both were not hungry enough for dinner and cancelled the reservation. They agreed to meet in the morning, in the dining room, and have a full english breakfast. Bette said, "we shall both be starving by then, especially after tonight (meaning, we suppose, not eating?).

The two spent two hours at the breakfast table. Both were ravenous and ate everything on the table; scooping out all the marmalade and jams from their miniature jars. Asking the waitress for more toast and butter and really taking advantage of the hotel special of two full english breakfasts at 25% off. Bette couldn't believe she ate two eggs, a lamb chop, two slices of gammon ham, and two fat pork sausages. Baked beans and home-fried potatoes were also wolfed down. The Burlington hotel lost money that day.

They found a quiet corner in the hotel lounge and sat next to a large coffee table with a yellow pad of writing paper Bette pulled from her bag. She drew a line vertically down the middle of the page and tore it off the pad. Passing it to Tom, she said, "This is an American method of determining solutions. It's called, 'The Benjamin Franklin Method'. I learned this from an American I was working for a million years ago. On the left side you write "Pros" and on the right side, the "Cons. Now then any subject we discuss, we each write down what we feel. If we like it then put the subject in the "Pros" column. I shall be doing the same on my sheet. This way we can look at each other's thoughts without worrying about voice inflection or tone, or sarcasm etc. Got it me old cock sparrow?" she said with a big grin.

"I call it the Tom Gale method," he replied with a wicked grin, "if anything appears under the "Cons" column, the whole thing is hopeless."

"What nonsense, "Bette admonished "now let's get on with it". Bette, of course, started, "First, I sell my flat. I have a buyer and the money will go into a private account. Pro or con?"

Tom said, "We live in my house until the show home is available."

Bette said, "We live in your house after we are married."

Tom retorted, "We could get married tomorrow."

The lounge and the bar were now beginning to fill up and Bette was getting flustered. "We can't work here, this is too important to keep being interrupted. Look at that one there, he's drinking a beer and its only noon. My God, its noon. Where has the time gone? Let's go up to my room. The view is wonderful and we will have no interruptions. Okay?" she stood up and left for the lift, with Tom right behind her.

Room 502 had been cleaned and was neat and tidy. There was a card table at the open window with two very comfortable chairs. Tom took his jacket off as Bette did with her cardigan, and they continued their exploratory quiz.

"Right" said Tom, "at the house, I'll park my car on the street and you can park yours in the driveway." Tom explained, "I like the left side of the bed."

Bette said, "I am exhausted, so after this I am having a nap. Then we can go home and chat with the boys. They are home aren't they?"

"No" said Tom, "they are at a football game and won't be home until about 1800. So we can nap here or there, whatever you wish, dear."

They went through a long list, and except for what time they preferred to go to bed, Tom preferred 2100, Bette, 2230. They agreed on everything. They were quite delighted to discover that both of them like toast with marmite. "Our breakfasts are going to be easy," said Bette "what do the boys like?"

"Breakfast, hah! Cold pizza out of the fridge or nothing, usually." Answered Tom with a grin.

Around two in the afternoon, both of them lay on the King sized bed and very slowly reached for each other's hand. They were asleep for nearly two hours. Both refreshed themselves in the bathroom and decided to drive to Tom's house and finish their talk in the car and at home until the boys got there.

"We could get married in the Elm Church," said Tom, "I shall drive by it so you can see what it looks like. Quite old and historic looking. Look, there it is," he pointed to his left. A lovely 18th Century grey stone classical design building, and right in the middle of town."

"Oh yes that looks fine," Bette replied. Now realizing that Tom had asked her to marry him, and she had, in a way, said yes. "When do you think might be best?"

"Lets see how many people and who they are, that we want to come to the wedding," said Tom. "Then we can start figuring out when they may be available and how long it would take and so on."

"Oh I can't be bothered by all that nonsense, let's just have my closest relatives and yours, and that's it. Family only. I shall sell my flat and vacate it by next month. I will drive down here quite often bringing my belongings in drips and drabs, so my last trip will just be a suitcase. So, it looks like maybe at least a month before we can get wed. How's that sound to you?"

"Hey my birthday is on April 11th. Let's make it that day. So two months from now, is that rushing it a bit?"

"Let's check the calendar and see if the church is available and I will say yes."

They pulled into the driveway of the house and carried on talking as they entered the front door Tom yelled for the boys but there was no reply. Tom held Bette for a moment, looked her straight in her eyes and said, "Welcome to your home. As of now you belong here," and kissed her with passion and Bette responded in kind.

The rest of the evening was to get as many questions settled about the simple logistics. Dates, times, places, who, where, what. All those items that need solving for a wedding and a life together. They were exhausted when the boys got home about 2030, covered in green grass stains on their shorts and mud everywhere, with a bit of blood in one nostril and a very black bruise under an eye. Just another football game by boys, in England.

"Oh hello Bette, " they said in unison, "we're going out in a while as there is a rock and roll party at the football club. See you around 2330, if you haven't gone by then. Byeee." The two rushed to be the first in the bathroom.

The 'inquisition" went on into the night. Bette wondering if Tom would make a move. Tom wondering what Bette would do if he did. As it was, he drove Bette back to the hotel around 2230 and she said goodnight, at the car, leaning in through his window and kissing Tom on the lips, "Goodnight dearie, " Bette said and went up to her room, where she slept like a log until 0800.

The problem with war is that you need to make quick decisions if you think your life is in danger. Too slow and you may never get anything done. Too fast and you could have many consequences. What if you just went ahead and made a big decision and to hell with any consequences, such as maybe I will be dead tomorrow so who cares. And then you aren't dead, you are alive and have to live with your decision every waking hour of your life. Having both been affected by war, these two people were very vulnerable and yet they learned one great truth: You cannot control one's life based on wishes and guesses. Even making decisions based on only facts does not guarantee they are the right decisions. Hell you might as well go through life and never make any decisions.

Bette knew she could walk away from it all right then. Pack her belongings and leave. She could phone Tom and tell him she was a coward and could not marry him. Tom could decide that Bette was simply not what he had assumed she was. He too could walk away. That evening and the next morning both had these thoughts racing through their minds. Worrying then going in another direction. What would happen after they walked away from each other?

The visits to the hotel and going to Tom's house, went on for about seven months. At least a visit a week and sometimes three days, sometimes just one. On one visit Bette checked into the Burlington hotel, arriving unannounced, by taxi from the station. Bette phoned Tom, announced she was at the Burlington hotel and asked if he would pick her up at the hotel, at three p.m., it was ten a.m.now. He agreed.

24

A NEW FRIENDSHIP

Bette asked for a taxi at the front desk and had the driver take her to the Elm Church on Broadwater Street. Bette had liked the look of this church so thought she would check it out. On a hunch, she felt better about this church and it was closer to her hotel than any other one. She hoped the minister would be there as she needed some impartial conversation.

She went in and noticed how cavernous it was inside, much bigger than it seemed from outside. It was not the usual stone inside, it was white and more modern. There were fresh flowers everywhere and there was a woman playing a hymn on the pipe organ, "Oh God Our Help In Ages Past". Bette sat down in a warm corner and listened to the music. All her memories came flowing back to her. Jack Simmons, then the bombing and the death of her mother and sisters. The kindness of David at the factory and the friendship from the members of the Vintage Car Society.

Then the woman stopped playing and walked over to Bette. "Hello," she said, extending her hand to Bette, "I am the new manager at this parish. Frankly, I should be a Vicar but while that is allowed in some parts of the world, the Anglican higher-ups, in England, still have politics and major masculine thoughts to overcome. Still, I had the role of a Vicar once, in Barbados. I was born right here and when my Father was transferred to Barbados to supervise a large hotel chain, of course I went too. Later the church thought I would be a good role-model in England, with over 20 years running a very large parish, ten times larger than this one. And here I am.

I believe, and so I am told, that I am a test of sorts. Will any parishioner care that I am a woman, or that I am in charge or will they hate me so much that they demand a male to run this outfit? Who knows, but so far it's early days and each and every interaction I have encountered. A, the subject has never been alluded to and B, the meetings were warm and friendly as well as productive. I must say it's not very busy you happen to be the first person to come in here today. Is there anything I can help you with?"

Bette said "Could you and I have a conversation over a cup of tea, somewhere? I have some doubts running amok and I need to get all my thoughts in a straight line so I can go through each one."

"Oh my. I am Sheila Burkett, call me Sheila. You do sound like you need a little sisterly advice. Come up to my flat and let's share a while together, shall we, there is nothing that a good cup of tea can't resolve."

Bette believed in God, but had never been religious. Churches were there for important events, such as funerals, weddings, christenings. She believed in all those events but never went to church regularly, just to go. She did like this lady Vicar, or whatever her title was, and she went up to a very cozy little single bed-roomed flat, adjacent and attached to the church, with a view of the ocean from the lounge window.

Bette said, on entering the flat, "Ooh look, your view is the same as I have out my Burlington Hotel window."

"Yes that's right. There's the Burlington down there just on our left," said Sheila, "now let me put the kettle on. Black Ceylon or Breakfast Tea, Bette, it is Bette, right?"

Both sat across from each other at a small table by the window. Sheila munched away at a pile of ginger snap biscuits, dunking each one carefully into her perfectly brewed Black Ceylon tea. Bette sipped her tea but ignored the biscuits. As they sat there Bette noticed that the tea cups were not a well known brand and Sheila had a small crack in her cup. Bette always made note of important details like that.

"So, tell me your dilemma," asked Sheila, "I have to pry to see if I have any ideas. You know anything you say to me here, or anywhere else for that matter, is between you and me only. Like a Catholic Confession. I'm assuming you are Anglican, being at my church today. Also many ideas may be from me as a woman rather than just the opinion of a church lady."

"You know," said Bette, "with all the horror in the world today. All the suffering. My problem seems so silly and really all I need is a shoulder to cry on, maybe to laugh on, it's hardly a problem." She went into a lot of detail about Tom and what her situation was then and her feelings about being with him. And her feelings about forgetting the whole idea and moving back to her contented previous life.

"My previous life was very satisfying but I can't see me fitting in to this community. I don't mean I don't like Worthing, but I don't know Worthing. I've had the grand tour and have seen the seaside and the housing estates, along with some fine buildings, but what is behind it all?"

"Bette what you are saying has nothing so much to do with Tom or his family or Worthing, it's your security and the "do I fit in?" question. I bet your circle of friends in London are many, and you can call on any of them when you are looking for a deal, or a helpful hint or anything. Someone will know someone and get you what you want. You do not know anyone here."

Bette nodded. Sheila continued, "So, what you need is a quick "welcome to Worthing, Bette, party" without anyone knowing it was that kind of party. I can arrange a party of some very nice and influential ladies of Worthing, and you could be one of the guests. So it's not really your party at all. Furthermore, if you had a particular hobby, or subject you would like to tell our guests about, we could put you on the roster one day."

Bette was very intrigued by this. She had been thinking that her life may have been somewhat geared to herself being content, at the expense of a more rounded and perhaps more satisfying life. She had been thinking of joining the local goodwill society. The one in London was a fund raising store that sold second-hand clothing, leather goods and household crockery, but only classy enough that the wealthy shopped there. The funds raised would be invested free and the earnings would be donated to the poor. Bette had imagined her being involved in that place, but now wondered if such a place could be found in Worthing. Sheila pressed Bette to explain the faraway look on her face just then, and Bette told her about her keenness for doing some charity work.

Sheila replied, "Bette, from what you have just explained, God has answered my prayers. There are not a lot of poor families in the area around Worthing, but then that is good as there is not a large population around here to support them. But I have an idea and I would help you as much as I have time to, and I can round up some more bodies to help. You see the Church trust has a building on a side street near the pier, It was a warehouse a hundred-ish years ago, and it has been put to many different uses since. It was a place for veterans to use after both world wars, like the first MOTH club (Memorable Order Of Tin Hats) but fewer and fewer men used it and so it has been closed for twenty years now. The church could sell it but nobody has been clamoring to buy it, and what would we get and what would we do with the money, invest it? And who would that be for?"

Sheila continued, getting very enthusiastic. "But if we could put it to good use, then the church would still own it and we would be using an asset better than simply selling it. Now imagine, Bette, it's about 4,500 square feet, with a basement and even a small attic, with strong open wooden stairs leading to both. We also have a bunch of workers who were paid to do some work for the church, before my time, and they owe us the deposit we supplied them to fix that hall. We closed it down before they could get started and now they are not able to round up the deposit money they owe us. We could get them to work it off by doing some carpentry and painting and cleaning over there. You could be head of the charity and arrange teams of people to get quotas, say one team rounding up clothing while another team collects crockery and cutlery and antique or valuable vases, figurines and so on. You would do the books and show them your management skills by going out with each team the first few times, to show how it's done and how to rob the rich to feed the poor.

Now then, Bette, beamed Sheila, "do you think you have the balls, oh sorry, yes the balls, to take that project and run with it, huh? You'd have to live here and get yourself known and if you missed London you could get there in under an hour, by car, just over, by train. But you might become so embroiled in your project here you might just forget to remember London at all. Oh yes, and Tom, just marry the bloke and you know he will be there for you forever and you have two boys who now and then could provide you with some hard labour for the charity. What do you think now, Bette?"

Ooh! Bette liked that. Her mind was racing, as she was already planning the job in her head. "Can we go and see the hall right now?" she asked. "It's only twelve thirty p.m. and we could spend twenty minutes there and drive back here. Oh no, do you have a car?" asked Bette, "mine is still in London but of course it will be here forever next time I come down, in a week I suppose."

Sheila said she had the time if they went right then, as she had a bunch of concerned citizens coming to a meeting at four p.m. Bette asked if she could use the phone, then phoned Tom at his office. "Hello dear, do NOT pick me up at the hotel at three p.m., as we arranged, come to the hotel at seven p.m., what's that, 1900 your time? Look at me getting all militarized and all that, hanging around you. We can eat at the hotel, Okay, thanks, I knew you would, yes, I know. Lots to tell you, ta ta."

Sheila and Bette both visited the bathroom, put a little make up on then their coats and they jogged downstairs to a little lean-to garage and got into the 'Vicar's' very fancy and brand new 1970 Volvo station wagon. Sheila could see Bette eyeing the car as she got in and said, "Church perk. Have many parishioners spread out and this church likes to visit people in their homes, especially when needed. Deaths, illnesses and regretfully, these days, more divorces."

It wasn't ten minutes and they parked on the street outside a plain brick two-storey building, almost windowless except for four small 15x20 inch panes at the top just under the eaves. Bette could see where a large shop window needed to be put in next to the front door, but kept that to herself for the moment. Inside was dusty and a bit of mildew, with piles of newspapers around the floor. If anyone paid more than £10,000 for this building they were doing so for the location. The building was sound but needed a good inspection and light, heating, air, complete window replacements and the new 10 X 7 foot, thick-glazed shop-front window. But both of them nodded in agreement that this was a perfect little jewel that would help the church and the poor, and certainly, Bette.

They drove back after less than fifteen minutes in the building. "Let's refer to it as Madeira27, its perfect. It's where it is so we'll never forget the address and hopefully neither will our customers," Bette suggested. Both were already referring to it as "ours" and as if it already existed. Fun times ahead.

They parted later, vowing to keep in touch. Bette gave Sheila Tom's office and home phone numbers, as well, for a while her Earl's Court flat number. Sheila handed Bette her card which had the words "Head Honcho" written next to 'Title' as well as her number. Sheila's meeting was not too far away and Bette's hotel was not much out of her way, so Sheila dropped off Bette at about three p.m.

These two had only met that day and it was as if their meeting was pre-ordained. They had become like twin sisters even though Bette was somewhat older than Sheila

Bette asked for a pad of writing paper at the front desk, then ordered some tea and biscuits to be sent up to room 502. Then she sat herself down at the table by the window, and started scribbling. She had not noticed that it was just after seven when there was a knock on her door; it was Tom. "Oh sorry Tom," said Bette, getting up, taking his raincoat and hat, and planting a kiss on his cheek. "I have so much to tell you and, it's all positive.

Now then, how hungry are you and do you want to get room service or go down to the dining room?"

"I think we could talk here, or you could talk and I can listen, much better up 'ere, so let's order for 'ere. "I could go for a cold beer and a roast beef sandwich, 'ow about you, my dear?"

"Well," Bette thought for a moment, "how about a shrimp cocktail and a cucumber sandwich, with one of their lemon tarts, and a Shandy? Then maybe go down for tea, later on?"

Tom got on the phone and ordered, "and throw in another lemon tart for me" then found the leather side chair and said, "I'll sit here until the food arrives and you start telling me all this stuff that's got you all excited."

And so she did. Explaining her whole day and the meeting and Sheila and the new opportunity to work at a business that would make her more fulfilled than rich. She laid out the wedding plans, the church where it would happen and the honeymoon, where that would be. "And no, I am not going to bloomin' Majorca or viva Espagna but I do want to go to Barbados. BOAC (the name changed to British Airways in 1974) has a special run in mid-week that is very affordable. I have had an offer to stay at a friend's family home, well Sheila, who I mentioned, the lady vicar at the church, well, it's her place for a week, so that will be fun. Then when we return I will be fixing up our house and in between working out the logistics of the charity, I will try to make the boys a higher priority over the charity, but I can't promise 100%.

On the other hand the boys are in their teens and don't want hand-holding by a stepmother all day long. They will fit in the easiest of all. To keep you and me out of each other's hair, and this is important, I will likely be out two to three nights a week, to attend to the charity and the social meetings associated with it. Sometimes, but not often, I shall need you with me to boost my confidence and so the people of Worthing can see my other half, and that would be you. We shall see how it goes, maybe less nights and only one but maybe two afternoons out, each week. I can't say what the arrangements will be and for sure they will be different each week, but as long as you agree, as understanding by you is crucial. Do you follow me?"

Tom smiled "Look girl, don't worry about anything. Whatever you want to do is fine by me. As long as I get you with me for at least 51% of the time, I will be a happy man."

The wedding date was chosen: April 22 1973, at the Elm Church, with Sheila Burkett presiding.

It was now mid December 1972, and Bette told the buyer of her flat that she needed it until her wedding. Slowly, with weekly drives down to Worthing, she moved all her worldly goods, and she certainly had lots of those, into Tom's house.

But she had asked Sheila if she could store a lot of household goods, crockery and cutlery, along with ornamental figurines etc, into Madeira27, until she could sort out where they fit. Of course Sheila agreed. A few days later a small moving van dropped off a few pieces of prized furniture at Tom's house, then before heading back to London, dropped off many boxes at Madeira27.

Sheila phoned one day and said, "Bette, remember when we started all this and I said we might have a party with you as a guest, well how about this coming Friday night?" Bette said yes immediately.

"Yes I am coming down Friday and staying at the Burlington, so would love to be there."

"Right, I'll book the church hall for the evening," replied Sheila. "But wait, maybe you could think of this, you are having the meeting to announce your new charity project and you give a speech as you are looking for first signer uppers to be directors along with you. Hey, whatcha think, girl?"

"You know that really is a good idea. How many people will you attract?" asked Bette.

"Well I thought of inviting certain women only, not a general invitation, and I think we want all of them to feel a strong part of the beginning. Get the movers and shakers on board at the beginning and no amount of any back biting will bring it down. Yes, you learn a lot in running a church, tee hee." Sheila said, wickedly.

Bette was very enthused but had only one negative thought, "Timing is important. I'm not sure I should be introduced as Bette Simmons and then within weeks I am Bette Gale. Should I give a damn or should we wait just a few weeks longer?"

"Oh really Bette, let's just get on with it. This week you are Bette Simmons and we explain why you are new in Worthing. Many knew Tom or his deceased wife, from her involvement in medical issues. I believe they would all like to think Tom is going to be taken care of and that you are a fitting replacement for his wife. Charitable business or not, there would be talk anyway. This way you take the bull by the horns and control the gossip. Friday then, say eight pm for two hours? I'll arrange the tea".

"Okay, Sheila, thank you, I think. I shall work on a speech, twenty minutes enough?"

"Perfect."

25

SETTLING IN

Perhaps the gods were on Bette's side that day, traffic jams were nowhere to be found. She left London at two p.m., just escaping the mad Friday early rush-hour of upper middle classes who simply had to get to the country for the weekend. Following the Thames River and listening to her favourite singer on the car radio, Neil Diamond singing 'Sweet Caroline", and her singing along. The Hillman Minx hummed and she was feeling very pleased with herself.

She was at Tom's house at just after four fifteen p.m. and both boys rushed out to help her unpack the car. Bette had dozens of boxes in every spare space in the car, and they placed them in the few remaining spaces in the house. Tom was at work. John and Richard went out after making Bette a tea, and she sat at the dining room table to take all her notes and put them on 3x5 index cards. She had done a lot of public speaking and learned the art of shuffling cards sideways across the lectern, rather than flipping 8x10 pages.

Bette decided that rich people would be shopping in her 'store' and the only items she wanted in that store would be first class, hardly used or worn, and labels that made your wallet flinch. The first items would be her own crockery. She had sets of Coalport and Royal Worcester Spode. There was Royal Doulton, some French Limoges, and a perfect little tea set by Royal Albert. Now that set she was giving as a gift to Sheila Burkett, who really needed a decent set, as hers was cracked. Then she wanted clothing that was high end, Burberry, Channel, and Gucci, and so on. She debated having men's clothing but chose female only, and hoped that there would be some gossip about that. Great advertizing.

Friday was suddenly there. Bette scrambled to look just right. She wore a two-piece woolen suit in a pale powdery lavender, and a high collar white blouse with lace trim. Medium-heel light tan leather shoes and matching leather handbag. She parked the Hillman in the spot Sheila had assigned for her, almost right at the front door. There was a hum emerging from the building as Bette strode in and walked over to Sheila, who was introducing two other women.

Bette held out her hand and Sheila grasped it with two hands. "Oh I am so glad you are here. We have twelve ladies and I would like to introduce you to all of them, so let's do the rounds."

The first woman was a mousy little thing, about seventy years of age and her yellow dress actually hanging on her frame. Her hair was snow white and in a bun. She had a classy style and was obviously stronger, healthier and more energetic than at first glance. "This is Dorothy Bladen, a friend of the church and a long-time resident, well you were born in Worthing were you not?" asked Sheila.

"Yes, I am afraid I am probably the oldest person here and born here before the pier was built," she smiled, "and who is this charming lady with you, Sheila?"

"Ah yes, this is Bette Simmons, who has just moved permanently to Worthing and is our guest speaker tonight."

Bette shook her hand and said, "I am going to have to read your birth certificate, that handshake felt pretty young to me. So pleased to meet you. Can we talk later?"

Sheila said, "Must be off to meet the others, see you later Dorothy," and tugging Bette's hand, she dragged her over to a small group of five women, seated at a sofa and a couple of dining chairs.

"Don't say a word, I believe I can remember all your names. Matilda Carson here, next is Joan Gooding, then Harriet Franks, Beryl Smythe and last Jennifer Wilson. Ladies, this is Bette Simmons, our guest speaker tonight and a new resident of Worthing." All the women made friendly gestures, waves, hand-shaking and nodding. Collectively they said, "Hello pleased to meet you and look forward to hearing what you have to say tonight."

Bette made a bee line for a table that had some tea and a few biscuits. She ignored the biscuits but found the largest cup, filled it with tea and milk, and three sugars, and stood there drinking it down and eyeing the crowd. Then she nodded at Sheila and asked her to introduce her to the last group of ladies sitting near the fireplace, which was not on as it was a mild evening.

Once Bette had been introduced, Sheila went up to the large table at the end of the room, on which was a lectern with a small brass reading lamp. She clanked the side of a glass vase to get everyone's attention: "Ladies we would like to commence this evening's short program. Many had asked me if they could escape, (lots of giggles over that word), I mean leave, by nine thirty p.m., and I believe we can if we get started now. It is eight fifteen now and Bette says she is ready, so, without further ado, bring your chairs up as close as you wish. If any need a bathroom break then go now and we shall wait. Three took advantage of the break and a few minutes later were in their seats.

Sheila stood up, all five-foot-one of her, and said, "I am so pleased to introduce our speaker tonight. We met a few months ago and hit it off wonderfully. I had an idea and wanted her opinion and she bounced back with her opinions, and what you will hear tonight is the result of those combined ideas. Please welcome Bette Simmons."

Bette began, "First let me thank you for volunteering to come and listen to a complete stranger and a newbie in Worthing, without any reputation for giving rip-roaring speeches. I know you didn't pay to hear me but you may well be poorer when you leave. I have an idea that will make this evening seem like a brainwave that should have happened a long time ago, but something called a world war stopped many ideas from progressing. I believe now is the time to make a fresh start.

I don't know how many of you know that the church owns a building on a side street off Marine Parade. It is at Number 27, Madeira Street. Sheila had the idea that the church might be able to sell it to increase the church bank balance, but then, she thought, what price would the church get for it and what would the money be used for? I must admit I had no suggestions. Then Sheila talked about using the building as a thrift shop and use the proceeds of the sales to help the needy. I have been involved in a number of charitable organizations and I jumped at Sheila's idea. The two of us went on exchanging ideas for a number of hours the first meeting. Then the many hours over the weeks and months we have been setting this up. I am excited about this plan and I want you to be excited too.

Sometimes we believe that a charity is simply a way to give help to someone less fortunate than we are, and it is, any donations will help. But I want us to also have fun dreaming up ways to make money and then use that money as best we can to help the poor. So, briefly, here is what I plan to do, but first off, I will need volunteers. Everybody involved in this business will work hard and enjoy it. Three women in this room tonight will become directors of the business and therefore will sit on the board, with Sheila, and me. They will have their ideas put forward and enjoy themselves at the same time.

I hope we can open the doors in about a month. That will give me time to get married to a Sussex gentleman called Tom Gale. Some of you may know him, he runs a house-building company here. At that, there was a slight hiss and a mumble from the audience. Tom and I have known each other since before the war, but really only got back together last year. My best friend since before the war, was Kitty Gale. Tom is her brother. He has two sons and has been a widower for nearly two years now. Once I settle down, and Sheila gives me the green light that the building has been spruced up, our business can begin.

In the meantime, we all need to start now with our efforts so that we are ready on opening day, and not just ready to be ready. We are going to have a first-rate classy store where above average income people, like us, can shop for the finest china and cutlery. Maybe an opportunity for someone to replace one saucer in a particular pattern or perhaps pick up an entire set of china, at far less than the typical price in other retail stores. Also, we will sell top-of-the-line clothing and shoes. Jewellery will also be featured.

What I propose is that we will donate anything we can, as a start, and then visit various people and businesses, to let them know we can help them donate to us. I can tell you from experience in London that companies like being able to write off a certain line of shoes or clothes so they can re-stock and we end up with new fashions, just not the very current edition. This can be done with many goods but I believe we should be more than a simple thrift shop and just stick to the three categories. I also want to have on hand the services of a fine jeweller, antique appraiser for crockery, and other such experts.

If any of you know any such people I would appreciate you telling me, not them. I found out the hard way what happens when word gets out too soon as to what we need. Here's what can happen: Let's say four of you each know a fine watchmaker. If you each tell them you want them in the business, then three are going to be awfully unhappy as we only want one, not four. We will interview each candidate and describe why we need them and explain why they will gain business by being associated with us. They will gain prestige when they show that they have been selected by the Madeira27 group as a consultant. They will be remunerated but we hope at a charitable rate.

So, I need someone to sign on as being the Director responsible for crockery and cutlery and household décor. Then I need someone responsible for jewellery, and a third for clothing and shoes. These three ladies will be our first Directors. Now I do not want a rush of hands I have forms here for all those interested to complete. We will be interviewing you within days and the chosen names will then be announced. Actually, if you are interested at all in just helping out then please complete the form and we can have it ready to call when we need you. Some people prefer to work behind the scenes, they like bookkeeping or just collecting and delivering items. Others may want to help out behind the counter when shoppers come in. All those positions are available and necessary and those people are often the backbone of any business, and we certainly need you. So, while I take a small drink of water, do any of you have any questions for me?" Well, as was expected all kinds of questions arose, all of them very positive and many contributing ideas of their own, which Bette dutifully wrote down.

One lady asked about musical instruments, "I have recently discovered that there are so many quite valuable instruments around. People who perhaps bought a fine guitar decades ago and gave up trying to play. That guitar could go to a young child whose parents simply could not afford that," suggested Dorothy Bladen.

Bette replied, "Let's not automatically accept or reject any ideas. Dorothy, how about heading up a committee to determine how many of each instrument might be out there, somewhere, and let's see if, in fact, there are quite a few. If there are many then perhaps we can move to Plan B. Could I leave that with you, then, Dorothy?" Dorothy nodded.

With a few more general questions from the ladies, the evening drew to a close. It was most definitely a success. With everyone in the room completing an application form and, some, adding names of others that might be interested in joining, Bette soon had her team with three Directors, and it was not long after that they were phoning and asking if they could store items at Madeira27. Furthermore, it turned out that a musician, Geoffrey Lastman, who had taught music in Worthing for over thirty years, and now wanted to retire, had a large supply of instruments he wished to donate. And so plan B came into effect. Madeira27 decided to set aside an annex in the building where, after store hours, or on a Sunday, they would form an orchestra for children six years of age and up to eighteen. The children would be selected from families under a certain poverty level, and each child would be subject to an audition. If Mr. Lastman could see a talent then they would be included.

If, in his opinion, the child had absolutely no skills and likely would never be able to play an instrument, then a polite decline, with a promise to audition again in one year's time.

Mr. Lastman wanted to retire from running a business but still wanted to have music and children in his life. He volunteered to drop by and teach the children twice a week from six to ten p.m. and even on Sundays from one p.m. to five p.m. Dorothy Bladen also worked out a deal with him where he could use the annex free to teach private lessons and then he could sell his old store, and live very comfortably on the proceeds.

While the behind the scenes activity grew each day, Bette was now also concentrating on her wedding. Of course she wanted all the trimmings and the right setting with the correct dress. Being business savvy and coincidentally absolutely lucky, she selected a wedding dress that had been donated to Madeira27 by a boutique that donated all its clothing line. The new owners were concentrating on becoming outfitters for items such as saddles, bridles, horsey type equipment and clothing. Bette paid way less than a similar dress but she also made sure everyone knew she had made the first purchase from Madeira27, even though its doors were not 'officially' open yet. Once people knew that the big-shot at Madeira27 had purchased her wedding dress from her store, then they too could be seen buying there. Marketing was always on Bette's mind.

Every shop Bette visited had a good deal of knowledge about Bette and the new charity shop and how they could benefit from the occasional donation; the word had spread. A few items were offered to Bette for her wedding but she refused to accept them. "I shall have one of my Directors call you and discuss various mutually satisfactory ideas," said Bette.

Her wedding to Tom was beneficial to her, from both the satisfaction and peacefulness of finally settling down and marrying Tom and his two boys. Also, the getting to know people and businesses in and around Worthing, because of her charity business, was so comfortable and pleasing. The week before the wedding Bette called Sheila and asked if she could join her in her flat for a cup of tea and a chat. Bette walked in carrying a small cardboard box and presented it to Sheila. "This is for you and I am giving it to you because you need it and you deserve it. You have become a very good friend and so this is also a friendship gift. It is a Coalport china four-piece tea set with four side plates, a teapot and a sugar bowl and cream jug. I do so hope you like it."

Sheila took each piece out of the box; marveling at the fine detail and colour of this hand-made piece of English history. "Oh Bette, you shouldn't have. This should be kept hidden away at home until the Vicar visits, and I would have, often. Look this must be 100 years old and it is exquisite. Thank you so so much." Sheila gave Bette a hug and said, "Welcome to Worthing. I believe you have started something here and all of us will benefit."

26

THE BIG DAY ARRIVES

Bette and Tom were married on a lovely sunny day in June 1973. She wore a dusty pink long sleeved dress, trimmed with a white wrap-around collar, and a very large matching pink bonnet. Tom wore a three-piece dark brown suit. There were 11 guests, including Tom's sons, Richard and John and Mary Swan (author's mother) as well as cousins and aunts, plus her great Aunt Florrie, sister to Bette's late mother, a fiesty seventy-eight year old. Her good friend now, Sheila, presided at the ceremony and then helped out at the reception after. Bette felt that she belonged in this community.

Tom and Bette had a friend drive them to Heathrow airport at 1900 hours, and caught a 0200 flight to Barbados. Sheila had given them her parent's old home, which she still owned after their deaths, and arranged for one of her old managers to pick up the wedded couple at Bridgetown airport and look after the couple for ten days.

The BOAC 707 jet landed in Bridgetown early in the morning. Sheila's property manager, Jeremiah, was there to meet them, and took their luggage and drove them to their small cottage, right on the beach, near Sam Lord's Castle. This was now a museum but back in the 17th Century, had been owned by Sam Lord who was a dastardly pirate, thief and murderer. Lord used to hang lanterns on the horns of his herd of deer, grazing on the hills, overlooking huge rocks. Seafarers thought the lights came from Bridgetown and headed straight for them. Sam Lord would send his men down to the wrecked ships and have the crew slaughtered. He then stole valuable goods and waited for the next ship to come along. Bette and Tom loved visiting Sam Lord's to examine all the fine china and other expensive items which he had stolen from various ships. Bette even asked if she could buy some of the china, but that idea was quashed right away by the curators.

Their cottage was quaint but needed Jeremiah to be there every day to help them shop for food, and learn how to eat various fresh fish, such as flying fish. They had rented a small car, a Ford Cortina, and toured nearly the whole island. From Nelson's docks to the second oldest parliament building in the world, then to Codrington college, lined with hundreds of perfectly planted trees, and visits to old sugar mills and rum distilleries. Needless to say, after sun bathing and swimming and eating very fresh and healthy food, neither wanted to return to England. But, BOAC was waiting, and a week later they flew out at 2300 hours, in a half empty 707, for an easy flight to London's Heathrow airport.

Arriving at 0600, they hired a taxi and they both slept in it until it arrived at the house, just outside Worthing, one hour later. Bette immediately phoned Sheila to report on their stay and on Jeremiah, and how nice he had been and how quaint the house was, and especially the small private swimming pool.

27

PEACE AND HARMONY

Just a few weeks later Tom came home beaming. "The last house sold today and I have asked my agent to get into the show home and get it ready and cleaned up for us to move into it in about two weeks. All we have to do is decide what day we arrange for the movers to get here and take our stuff over there. What do you think of that, my sweetheart?" He said very proudly.

Bette was delighted. This house was nice, but it wasn't hers, and she intended to make the new one hers. She got up and gave Tom a big fat kiss on the mouth and said, "There, see what you get when you make me happy?" Tom just beamed.

The doors of Madeira27 opened three weeks later on August 1, 1973, and it was filled with only the best of the best. No cracked crockery here, no scuffed boots or shoes. No clothing that had any repairs or odd buttons. All items were first class. In fact, the ladies picking up and delivering had a rough time obeying the rules. The rules simply stated that when you were first picking up, then reviewing and delivering items, you were not allowed to pick out what you wanted and simply make up what you thought was a fair price and keep the item. ALL items had to be sorted in the store, a price decided upon at the store, and then put on display. If you absolutely had to have a particular piece you couldn't say so because the price may be affected by them knowing you wanted it.

Reluctantly, but understanding the reasons, everyone eventually obeyed the rules. You had to act fast however, if more than one wanted the same item. Still, it was in good fun and the cash was flowing. Apparently, there are quite a few wealthy people in Worthing. There was a small queue outside the doors on the first day of opening. On the second day, word of mouth had the queue almost around the block, with ladies all waving chequebooks and wallets. Madeira27 became very profitable and sustained the reputation and success from the outset. Women loved shopping in there and many used the store as a meeting place as well as the place to be seen.

Bette loved her life. Finally a mother and a wife as well as a leading business woman. She never forgot her experiences during the war but they no longer affected her. She and Tom were happy, and happiest on motor tours around England. Between the two of them they must have seen every castle and cathedral ever erected in England. They never planned, they simply drove until they were losing interest. They always checked into the finest hotels, had a fine meal and lots of rest. Then do it all over again the next day, just driving somewhere else.

Similarly, Bette loved her independence when at Madeira27, socializing with women who had become good friends. The business meetings and the scheming to improve what they had but also to venture into other ways to help the poor. One could wonder how this small city in beautiful Sussex had ever functioned before Bette came along. She, of course, would never say such a thing. She liked everyone to know it, or think it, but she was too classy to even think it herself.

Bette managed to have some prominent jewellers, agree to appraise items donated at no cost to Madeira27, in exchange for having business referrals shown their way. Bette had the music man teaching children and not having to worry about running a business. He was so excited he actually forgot that he had originally wanted to retire. He was making money now as well.

One of Bette's good friends from London and a prominent member of the Veteran Car Society, decided to retire in Worthing. He bought Tom's old house at a deal that impressed him so much that he became a friend of Tom's and they met often and talked World War II and cars all day.

Two very charming Sisters, twins of sixty-four years of age, had donated much of their inventory of fine ladies clothing, when they heard of Bette's charity. But, while they had wanted to retire from their "downtown fashions" business, they had little to do now. They didn't miss running the business at all, but missed the interaction with customers. Both ladies had trained as seamstresses and designers in Paris when in their twenty's. Bette offered them a corner of the building at Madeira27, where they could help buyers modify any clothing that didn't fit just right, to adjust it so that it did. Their little business was easy, charge £5 an hour and pay Madeira27, £2. Then, if they wanted to invite the customers home for private fittings, anything charged there they kept.

One day the music man, Geoffrey Lastman, a very conservative man of average stature but with hair almost long enough to make a pony-tail, and a wicked sense of humour, approached the board and asked if he could form a choir. Many of the children, playing in his newly formed orchestra, had siblings who wanted to do something with music but didn't want to play an instrument; they wanted to sing.

He said he could easily round up twenty children from ages seven to eighteen. He had studied as a choirmaster a long time ago at Chichester College. His idea was that the children would be taught free of charge. Madeira27 would pay for their costumes and travel arrangements and the ticket revenue would go back to Madeira27, with the excess being invested for the charity. Parents of the children would accompany them with no costs to them for anything, including travel.

"Yes", he explained, "paying for the travel of two parents and one child may seem expensive, but Madeira 27 would have had to pay out a lot for supervisors, and besides which, I have a small bus company whose owners would like to become involved, somehow and they are willing to do UK travel at cost, as their way of contributing. I think it is a win, win and we should do it."

The Board approved it that night, subject to Mr. Lastman providing a satisfactory report a month before the first concert. Geoffrey was delighted, he seemed to be now an energetic young man, making money and still very involved in music. A few months later, the Board and invited friends and parents of the musicians, were invited to a concert with just the orchestra. Sheila arranged the church hall along with one hundred borrowed seats she had scrounged from a party organizer.

This first performance was by a chamber orchestra, because there were only forty three people playing. A full orchestra requires a few more woodwinds and two or more Brass instruments, such as French Horn and a Trumpet. The percussion section was well equipped, with one of the kettle drum players being a cute freckle-faced ten year old boy, who needed to stand on a box about eight inches high for him to look the part and swing the sticks. His dad was a carpenter and had measured up the requirements and built his son his music 'standing box.'

The very first piece, played outside of lessons, but not really to the full public, was Pachelbel's Canon in D Major. Mr. Lastman introduced himself and asked the first Violin to stand and take a bow, "Our First Violin," (a sweet brunette aged 14) "Deborah Fisher, thank you, Deborah." And with a tap, tap, on his lectern, Geoffrey turned that room into a magical, hauntingly magnificent chamber of music. Parents, who may have been only in their late twenties themselves, and who likely had never listened to much more than the Beatles and similar groups, were becoming very emotional. Some swaying gently to the music and wiping a tear away. Of course, the first tears were for the joy of seeing their child actually playing an instrument. But the second tear and the many that followed was for the beautiful sounds that emanated from those instruments, collectively.

Then when the thunderous and extended applause died down at the end, the orchestra swung into "Colonel Bogey", which almost had everyone wanting to get up and march around, the timing and the sharp notes, being very professional. Then Glenn Miller's "In the Mood", and back after that to Vivaldi's "Four Seasons". After young Deborah Fisher's solo, the crowd went crazy and Mr. Lastman had to implore them to stop.

The final piece was a theme from a film, "The Big Country" which really needs a full symphony orchestra with at least twenty violins to start the opening. There were only seven, but the children played with such energy and with such good training from Mr. Lastman, nobody missed a few extra violinists. Bette had dragged Tom down and he was one of the most excited people in the audience. He had also brought down his new friend, Lawrence Weaver, who had bought his house. Weaver was well off and had a sharp business mind. He couldn't wait to tell Bette what his idea was.

When it was all over the musicians had lots of hot chocolate to drink, along with dozens of assorted biscuits to gobble down. They were fine musicians but they were still ravenous and typical kids, soon the audience started filtering home, along with the child and the instrument. One parent, Charles Osborne, father of Henry, the clarinetist, suggested that while they could not afford much themselves, if they could get some type of backing from Madeira27, such as small envelope printed with something like, "Worthing's Charity for Musical Instruments."

The City needs the orchestra and we need a few more instruments. Please donate to the fund."

"With that showing it was legit," said Mr. Osborne, "I'm sure we could round up a few quid here and there. Maybe I could get other parents to assist? Maybe we need fifty of those envelopes?"

Typical of Bette she replied "Mr. Osborne, thank you so much for your suggestion. Just do it. Drop by in a couple of days and I will have those fifty envelopes printed for you. And then, young man, why don't you head up your own little group and become the head man for funding instruments, or maybe finding old instruments, in auction houses or estate sales?" Once again Bette had used common sense and her intelligence to get things moving along, with all kinds of people working at various chores and loving it; her too.

28

MORE IDEAS

Lawrence approached Bette and asked where he could get a decent cup of tea. She was standing right next to the teapot and poured him one. "Still no sugar then, Larry?" asked Bette of her old London friend.

He smiled, nodded and said "Bette, I noticed that the orchestra did not have a permanent place to call their own. Can I suggest that there is a building quite near here, in the next block actually, and I need a big tax write-off this year? I disposed of a bit too much when I came here from London. The building itself is useless, in fact I cannot think of anything it would be useful for. It is about 90 feet wide and 110 feet long. It's completely empty, just a small toilet and a sink in it. I was wondering if we could have the choir and the orchestra share the building. Only one door and two windows, too small and too high for break-ins. I would buy it and fix it up and donate it to Madeira27. I would get a write off so I would be happy and you would be able to divide your venture into a most obvious split. I know the music side was a last thought. So, watcha think, me ol' Darlin'?"

"Ooh you silver-tongued devil you," replied Bette. "You've talked me right into it. Now I need to know there will be brand new and working toilet and sink, in a lockable room from the inside only, right? Then I envision a small walled off area with a small kitchen, where you say there is another sink now. Nothing much bigger than say forty square feet. And we need a fridge for all the little buggers, oops, children's, drinks and snacks. But I want to get on board a businessman here who sells large appliances and plumbing fixtures, so don't go paying full retail for those, not yet anyway, alright? And the sooner the better because I believe this orchestra business and the choir are going to really help Worthing. Firstly, it'll keep the kids off the streets and secondly, it may well pave the way for all of them to pursue a career in music and having a bloody good time while they are doing so."

Ironically the address of the building was on Hubert Street, No 27. Bette was telling Sheila what she had done, over a nice cup of tea, in an exquisite tea service. "The church now has two buildings and I have named the second one, Opus27, so everyone will associate that building with music and Madeira27 as the shop. Like it?" she asked.

"Like it!" Sheila screamed, "I love it…go on, for that, you can have the last McVities Chantilly Cream Biscuit."

The following day, in a bar downtown, Larry found a whole bunch of men who had been let go just a week before, from their construction job. He heard one of the men moaning about their plight and he sauntered over and said, "Look, gentlemen, I have just bought a warehouse right downtown and it needs, plumbing, painting, a couple of concrete block interior rooms and so on. I will pay £5 an hour, each, for five men to start tomorrow and work two days. I will buy any material needed, such as appliances, fixtures and concrete block. You will need your own tools. There's not much parking around there but three cars, that's your two and mine, would fit. Okay?"

The five men all showed up on a Wednesday morning, as agreed, at seven a.m. One of the men in the Bar, Lefty Higgins, a scruffy Welshman with a firm handshake and overalls nearly falling off, had assumed the role of foreman. Larry had arrived at six forty five a.m. and was pleased that they had all shown, and on time. Lefty gave Larry a list of necessities, along with warnings such as "Make sure the flippin' fridge is no more than 32 inches wide. And the kitchen sink must be one that drops in over the counter and is stainless steel. Also we all like McVities biscuits, and Lyon's tea, along with milk and sugar you need about a hundred cardboard cups and a bag of plastic spoons. Cheers, matey, and thanks."

Larry then drove off to pick up Bette and she directed him to the appliance store. Naturally, she got a deal. She paid half the listed price for the fridge and got everything else free. They would be installed by the firm in three days, and forever more, that company would have small advertisements on Bette's new newsletter she had just thought of. Anyone receiving the newsletter could call Knapp's Plumbing and Appliances and get 10% discount off anything, any time of the year. Larry's jaw didn't relax for hours after watching Bette's transactions that day.

As Bette was leaving, she called out to the appliance man, "And don't forget the tap in the kitchen must have a spray arm on it, otherwise we will never get the kids to clean up. By the way, you and your wife will be our very first guests when we play our first concert later in the year."

Friday morning the hall was completed to Larry's and Bette's satisfaction, and each man was paid their agreed-to fee, plus a little extra because Bette wanted rows of small cupboards so that each child would have a locker with a combination lock in which they could store whatever they wished, but mostly accessories for their instruments. That was quite an expense: over £300 for labour and almost £100 for material. Bette decided to buy the kids a combo lock each, but that was another £70 for fifty locks. "Anyway," Bette scoffed, "better to do it right the first time". So, the final bill was £9570, and that included the building. Larry was very pleased with himself and Bette and Sheila, delighted. Geoffrey Lastman over the moon, and the kids, well let's say it was as if they had won an ice cream cone a day for life.

In October 1973, the choir and the now, fifty-two member Orchestra, performed at the Worthing Concert Hall, Opus27 needed to pay £1 for renting the building as an ancient law, still on Worthing's City Ordinance, which would not allow anyone to use the hall free. The Mayor could make the fee anything, and so £1 it was. The tickets were available for everyone, and the hall could seat 450 people. Parents and a handful of guests, including of course, Mr. and Mrs. Knapp, the appliance man, who, naturally, paid nothing.

The choir, surprisingly was not all girls, as had been assumed from the onset. There were thirteen girls and nine boys. The girls wore costumes that were fashionable for the times, but still looked a little like bridesmaids in powder blue. The boys all wore grey flannel trousers with a white shirt and an Opus tie, which they had custom made, and which were available at the booth in front, for a sum of £1. The tie was shiny black material with a silver music page and bars embroidered on it.

The orchestra filed in and all the women wore black, with a small musical logo on the left shoulder. The men wore the same as the men in the choir. Mr. Lastman bowed to the crowd and then sharply turned, held both arms high, and brought them down with vigour. The chorus hit a high note and the orchestra commence with a beautiful rendition of "Ave Maria". Six popular selections followed.

With nearly a sellout, some 440 in the crowd, clapped and bravoed every time they could. With tickets at £1 each, and minus the expenses incurred for the costumes, Opus27 was only £600 in the hole, and nobody was concerned. They would be in the black after the next two concerts.

Bette was very pleased with all that had happened in the months since her charity had started. They had raised a lot of money, over £30,000 net. Most of the money came from ladies clothing. Many women could not shop every week in London and yet here were fashions from London as well as Europe, and they wanted some. To buy a Burberry coat in London, for example, would set one back about £125. Yet right in the Madeira27 store, one was snatched up for £40. A pair of soft-leather winter boots, could be bought for a third of the new price, or less. Selling such fashionable clothes was easy, but making sure a steady supply came in regularly, was the main reason a lot of charities went under. Bette had seen that happen in London and found out why, and put in place systems to prevent it. Thinking ahead at least six months, constantly finding sources of supplies, always putting on display the best 60% of what you have and keeping a supply readily available as an emergency.

Tom taught her that. He told her about why the Germans had lost so many battles: they put everything they had into a fight. Great strategy if it was quick and you could plan another fight soon. But, if the enemy engaged you for sustained periods, you ran out of food, fuel, manpower, equipment and ammunition, and then it was too late. Finding new additions for Madeira27 while apparently always able to display plenty of fine items was a fine balancing act. Bette and her Directors did it.

Bette managed to balance her life about 70% with Tom and the boys. Going on weekend trips and then getting involved with the boys. Always being there to answer questions and guide them in strategies for getting through life, was what she did best. Helping with their homework was not her comfort zone. She taught all the men in her household how to cook. Not gourmet soufflé's or crepe susette, but basic pies, and stews, and eggs and bacon. Even taking four different tins of food from the pantry and experimenting how to make a tasty meal. She relished her role as mother and wife. She did say that motherhood was so much easier when not having to deal with "bottles, changing nappies and using car seats." The rest of her life was Madeira27.

29

CHANGES

Bette was thoroughly enjoying her life. Tom was certainly enjoying his. The two boys loved them both. Bette was happy to be at each boy's wedding, a few years later, and able to watch their families grow. Bette doted on everyone because finally she had a real family that she felt part of. Bette did say, "When those boys moved out to start families of their own, it was with mixed feelings as I waved goodbye. The home just seemed so empty. On the other hand they were not moving far away and now the number of family members had increased, quite a bit as time rolled on."

After such dismay and turmoil in their early war years, Tom said he would have preferred not to go through what he did. He also says he would not have missed it for the world. Bette said, "you silly old fool, there is nothing I miss at all."

They lived together for 25 years, in that same show home, until Tom passed away with prostate cancer, which he fought tooth and nail for five years, until 1998. A small funeral was held, with son's Richard and John attending, and Bette, trying so hard to be calm. Sadly they said their goodbyes to Tom, one fine man and a first-rate veteran soldier. Bette would have surely died of heartbreak had it not been for John and Richard who kept in touch often. They would visit Bette or have her over to their homes, which Bette relished.

Also she had so many friends, who respectfully left her alone, initially, except for regular visits from Sheila. Bette survived and then really threw herself into Madeira27 and Opus27.

30
OPPORTUNITIES

Five months later, Bette was chatting with a prominent London Doctor, who had dropped in to Madeira27 with his mother who lived near Worthing. They were on the prowl for some fine china for a gift for a friend. Bette happened to be in the store and invited both to sit down with her and have a cup of tea. She discovered from the specialist that men who had suffered strokes could often be almost 100% rehabilitated if they could be trained to sing, especially in a choir. Remembering words and holding notes, along with regular mental exercises and the camaraderie of fellow singers, all seemed to contribute to their rehabilitation. Bette soon saw another opportunity.

She consulted with various specialists, in London as well as locally, and it was decided that without making guarantees, no harm would be done if she was able to form a choir for these men. Subsequently, she and local hospitals and some physicians, along with Geoffrey Lastman, provided candidates and they were able to recruit, twenty men from various institutions. Each was taught to sing, alone at first then with others. Amazingly after just six months of training, the twenty man choir performed the song "The Hills Are Alive", from The Sound Of Music, before a 'Families only' concert. Six months later they performed two songs, at a public concert, "Yesterday", a Beatles hit, and again, by popular demand, "The Hills Are Alive " even joining in with the regular choir for another two songs, both love songs, "Please Release Me," made popular by Engelbert Humperdink, and, "I'm 'Enery The Eighth I Am," a tune by Herman's Hermits. The audience went ballistic. They stood and they cheered and would not stop applauding. Once again, publicity attracted more people to future shows and to Madeira27, thus continuing the cycle of donations, purchases and performances. All the while helping the community at every conceivable level. The entire choir took a bow. One could see the posture and the confidence each man had. Whatever the definition was of 'recovery', these men were much better than they were a year ago. Friends and relatives, including physicians, all swore that the changes and improvements were remarkable.

Bette missed Tom in her private moments, but she had few of them. She only had one problem and that was trying to keep up with her 'mini empire,' while sticking her nose into each department and trying to be not too bossy. She did not hold back, however, if she witnessed something she didn't like, or could see a better way of doing things. Nobody got mad at her. Everyone accepted what she suggested and the entire charity breezed along making money.

They had many successes with recipients of the charity's funds. One couple lived on a quarter -acre plot, but now could not afford to fix their home and could not pay their taxes, and the Government agency suggested they cede their home to them, and the government would find them a home for seniors and let them live out their lives, 'free'. One of Bette's directors discovered that many years before, this couple raised hens and sold eggs. Madeira27 swung into action. They determined the couple were quite healthy and if financed, could raise chickens and sell eggs again. A builder was hired and paid for by Madeira27, and he and his gang consulted with the old farmer as to the type and location of the chicken coop, and so on. Bette got a local organic grocer to buy their eggs, at a fair price. A year later the grocer was getting twenty-five dozen eggs a day, and the farmer was living with a small profit each month and, very proudly independent. Taxpayer's money was saved and everyone was a winner. Bette was proud of this.

She was always afraid that, like many charities, people became dependent on the free handout. The recipient would buy cigarettes and alcohol with the money and got sicker on their diets of potato chips and baked beans with a sausage now and then.

Bette looked for ways to donate funds if the recipients agreed to various requirements. Come in and get lessons on nutrition and how to cook on a low budget. More incentives if anyone gave up smoking and attended her BA classes (Bette Anonymous) for stop smoking ideas as well as helping out at the charity. She believed that people could change any habit if they were provided with another habit. Painting doll houses perhaps, or repairing and reconditioning old bicycles, helping deliver items to and from Madeira27. If they had any skills then Bette would try to get it incorporated into that person's rehabilitation.

This activity was everywhere. Notices in the newspaper; annual statistics: such as "Madeira27 has over sixty-five people working, one way or another, for the charity." Or, "last night's concert raised over £4,000, which brings the Madeira27 total income for the year to over £63,000. £93,000 was provided just for last year, to over thirty-eight people, and eleven more are being added next year."

The whole venture became a part of Worthing and Bette was the go-getter, with everyone happily working at minimum wage or donating their time, and exceedingly proud and pleased to be involved.

Seven years after Tom's passing, Bette had to step down as, what she called, "Numero Uno", because she had to stop driving. Her car, by now a 1995 Rover 75 Sedan, was fine, but Bette's eyesight was blurring and the police could no longer forgive her for some awkward scrapes, involving mostly other people's parked cars. Bette always paid for any damage and could well afford to do so, but the Head Constable called around one afternoon, asking for a cup of tea and a chat. "Mrs. Gale," he started, "giving people bad news is one of the most feared duties a policeman can ever face. Not one of my force ever dared to give you a ticket. The first one to give a ticket to Mrs. Gale would have been sent out on an ice flo, like the Eskimos do with their ailing relatives.

But you are now at a stage where we believe the licence bureau will be asking to pull your licence. I am here to give you advance warning of this and I suggest you sell your car and send in your licence today, by registered mail, and tell them you are surrendering it. There will be no publicity, as there would be otherwise, and the money you get from your car will be more than enough to use on taxi's. I am sorry to bring you this news."

"Oh, what nonsense," retorted Bette. "Thank you for your concern and the way you tried to break the news gently, but I have already sent my licence in, see, I am always steps ahead, Mr. Chief Constable. Now, how about a slice of cinnamon tart, which is the new favourite at Madeira27? And another tea?" She waved and smiled sweetly as the chief drove off.

And so it was that Sergeant Robinson of the Worthing Police Detachment came calling on Bette, that very afternoon, and asked, "Could I have first option to buy your car, when you decide to sell it, that is Mrs. Gale? I have looked up the Blue Book and I have an idea what a fair price is," he said.

Bette grilled him and said, "But you don't know what condition it is in or the mileage"

He replied, "Well, I do know the mileage, because I recorded it three weeks ago when you hit that car on the sea front parking spot, and it wouldn't be very much higher now, would it? And as for the condition, well, it's owned by Mrs. Elizabeth Gale, would it be any less than perfect?"

"Ah yes," said Bette, fully aware that she was being schmoozed. "I thought I recognized you and alright, I say it's worth £4,000, is that too much?"

"Well I am a Copper, and I say that's not enough. It is a Rover 75 and it has all the top options on it, with very low mileage of 23,000 miles. So really, you should be asking £6,500 and I would counter at £5,500, and then we would settle at £6,000. I'm not a car dealer but I gather that's how it's done. I hope I haven't offended you, or anything"

"How can you afford to pay for it?"

"I can get a loan at the bank and their interest rate is only 6%, so a lump sum to you."

"Alright" said Bette "You pay me £5,000 and I will charge you 2% interest, and you give me a series of post-dated cheques, for thirty-six 36 months at £147 a month. Can you afford that or would you like a longer term?"

"Wow! that is marvelous. My family will be delighted, but why such a deal for me?"

"Well I haven't finished with you yet. I may call on you to help my charity, when you are off duty." Bette said. "Okay?"

"Done" beamed Sgt Robinson. 'When can I pick it up?"

"You go and get the car cleaned out of all my stuff in it. Find the papers in the glove box, then go to your station and recruit a driver and bring him back anytime so you can drop off my cheques and sign the papers and you can drive it home. Is tomorrow Okay?"

"How about two hours from now?" He grinned.

Three hours later Bette stood at her bay window watching her Cobalt Blue Rover drive out of her drive-way. She sobbed, now that she was alone, at the finality of it all. Now she had to walk to the Post Office and mail her licence in. She had not already done so as she had fibbed to the Chief Constable.

31

RELUCTANT RETIREMENT

Every day for a week she called a different taxi company, auditioning each one: their attitude on the phone and how many rings before they answered; how long it took them to arrive and what was the driver like, and did the car live up to her standards. In other words, did it reach her 'snob' value.

The first driver was a smoker. Bette would not even enter his cab. "Go away, I don't want to smell like you," she said, quite haughtily. He wasn't too happy at that but did not feel like arguing with Bette, so he revved his engine and left. The second one, an hour later, had his own cell phone in the cab. He answered immediately and his voice had a smile. He answered politely and was in Bette's driveway just eight minutes later. Bette liked him and he took her down to Madeira27.

"Here's my card Mrs." he said, "Call me anytime, any trip, no minimum distance and no maximum. You are that Lady what started the charity, so all my fares will be 10% less than the meter, and no tip required. My name is Charlie Hatfield."

Bette tried three other taxi firms, and they were alright, but Charlie Hatfield was the clear winner. She had replaced her car for Charlie, and that seemed a good deal to her. She never used any other taxi again, unless Charlie was away or ill, neither of which he was, very much. The next time she called Charlie she said, "Look here my man, you have to make a living so no deals for me understood. I may use your help if I need something for the charity, and, I shall tip if you deserve it. Right then, understood?"

"Yeah, alright then," was his reply.

Tom's sons, John and Richard offered to take Bette to anywhere she needed to go, and Bette was appreciative, but she liked Charlie's attitude and enjoyed his company during her, mostly, short rides. Money was not really an issue for her.

Bette still attended Board meetings and worked hard until 2003. She resigned on her 90th birthday, in April. There was an enormous party, and all the Madeira27 orchestra and choir, including the men, along with customers, guests, employees and the Mayor, attended. And of course, Charlie in the back of the room, waiting to take Bette home. Bette enjoyed her 'retirement' as John and Richard's families were often visiting, and her nieces and nephews had children also visiting, often dragging along the great grand nieces and nephews. Plus, she and Sheila visited at least twice a week. But she also had a huge TV and enjoyed dozing off in front of it, as she enjoyed all those programs about how other people lived. "How boring my life has been compared to some of these people on TV," she would say. "When Tom was alive he would remark on the adventures the soldiers had on TV. "Bloody hell, the war I had was nowhere near as exciting as what these blokes are experiencing." He would say.

Little did they know how exciting and different their lives had been from the average person who lived during their time.

32

SHE DIDN'T LIKE TO BE TOLD

In 2009 Bette was forced to sell her house as she could no longer take care of it herself and even though she had installed a staircase lift, she was in danger of losing balance. A sad day for Bette. She had already completed her research, knowing this day would happen, so there came the day she had to be taken to an assisted-living home. The home she went to was superb, after all she had chosen it It had round the clock help and terrific meals. She was placed on the main floor, in a suite with a view of the Ocean, from her living room. The suite was bright with five rooms, totalling 900 square feet. She liked the place. But the loss of independence and, she said, the choice of TV channels, was ruining her spirit "and they don't know how to make a good steak and kidney pud," were the last words I heard her say, on my last visit a year before she died.

On my birthday, August 24 2010 at the age of 96, my Aunty Bette passed away peacefully. The funeral was as well attended as her 'retirement' party. Both of Tom's sons, Richard and John, and their families, were present. Sheila, now a seventy-two year old Vicar, and Bette's companion almost daily since Tom had passed away, officiated at Bette's funeral. They closed down Madeira27 for one day so all staff could attend. That was the Directors decision. Bette would never have allowed that to happen.

Sheila barely managed to get through the brief ceremony and then she almost ran to her car and left. She said afterwards, "I have had to perform many duties and many were extremely sad but, today, was the toughest job I have ever performed." Tears streaming down her face, she was unable to attend the reception.

And so, they are gone, Tom and Bette. During their life they just tried to get by without rocking the boat. The war was thrust upon them and they had to deal with it, as did millions of others. They surely accumulated more adventures than the average citizen during that war. They were of a different era, one of different values. Certainly today we should recognize that World War II veterans are almost extinct. The people of today really have little idea what these past generations had to do to survive. Furthermore they do not really understand what life today would be like, had Hitler won.

Let all of us be thankful that people like Bette and Tom joined with millions of others who sacrificed everything to stop Hitler.

33

PHOTOGRAPHS

The streets of Calais – During the battle
May 22 1940 – May 26 1940

Bette Swan marries Jack Simmons. Sisters Edie and
Lily are bridesmaids. Bette's Mother on her left

Bette 1935 studio picture

Bette in 1936 enjoying back garden

Memorial for 1940 battle, in Calais

Tom, the businessman, after the war

Bette, riding shotgun, in a 1952 Vintage
rally from London to Brighton

The tattered remains of the Cape Argus
newspaper, outlining Tom's heroics.

Bette posing for studio photograph in 1935

Bette and Tom's wedding in 1973.
Tom's sons, John and Richard, far left

ABOUT THE AUTHOR

Ken Swan was raised in South Africa and Northern Rhodesia, where he became a Police Officer. The political winds of change encouraged him to move and thrust him into the night life of London. He wanted to do something different than others. He won an audition on TV's "Opportunity Knocks" and was due to appear in January of 1966, but he decided, instead, to live a life of adventure and travel.

Since arriving in Canada in 1965, Ken made a living in the Employee Benefits business, but his life was wrapped around Amateur Theatre, obtaining his flying licence, making TV commercials, and meeting Hollywood greats, and not so greats, as a movie extra. Ken then took up watercolour painting and, since retiring from the insurance world, he is now a travel agent and a new author.

Ken is happily married to Helene. They have no children. They live in White Rock in British Columbia.

CPSIA information can be obtained
at www.ICGtesting.com
Printed in the USA
LVOW04s1313120416
483209LV00009B/19/P

9 781460 271735